EPISTLE to the AMERICANS I

What you don't know about the Income Tax

Copyright © 2009
by
David E. Robinson

Maine-Patriot.com
3 Linnell Circle
Brunswick, Maine 04011

maine-patriot.com

EPISTLE to the

*"Thus speaketh the Lord God of Israel, saying,
Write thee all the words that I have spoken
unto thee in a book."* — *Jeremiah 30:2.*

EPISTLE to the AMERICANS I

Patriots progress slowly for fear of being thought rediculous.

EPISTLE TO THE
AMERCANS
I
CONTENTS

Appendix

EPISTLE to the AMERICANS I

EPISTLE
TO THE
AMERICANS
I

CHAPTER 1

DAVID, a servant of Jesus Christ by the will of God, unto the believers in the American Republic.

2 Grace be unto you and peace from God our Father, and from the Lord Jesus Christ; I thank my God upon every remembrance of you.

3 Each year, millions of Americans scramble to meet the Internal Revenue Service's deadline for filing income tax returns.

4 Think about the millions of hours of productive time these forms waste.

5 Think about the outrageous intrusion into the personal affairs of Americans these rules cause.

6 Think about the inherent unfairness of a tax system that applies different standards to different people based on their income.

7 Think about the government's unspoken threat of force and violence and terror that accompanies this process.

8 Think about how little Americans have to say about the current tax system today.

9 Think about how government wastes, misuses and illegally redistributes the revenue it collects.

10 Think about how the system confiscates your wealth before you even see it, by forcing employers to do the government's dirty work.

11 Think about how some people are forced to pay up to 45 percent of their income to the government.

12 Think about how little Americans know — or could possibly know — about a tax code written by lawyers *for* lawyers, encompassing thousands of pages that few could digest in a lifetime of study.

13 Think about how almost 50 percent of the American people have been dropped completely from the tax rolls, while the other half is forced into indentured servitude.

14 Think about how our confiscatory tax system has forced millions of homes to send both

parents into the workplace and turn their kids over to be wards of the state schools and MTV.

15 Think about how Americans are conditioned to accept all this blindly, like sheep led to slaughter.

16 Think about all this, not just today, but every day of the week.

17 It's past the time for Americans to wake up, rise up and say "No more; enough is enough; we demand our government back!"

18 It's time for a new declaration of independence; it's time for rebellion; it's time, frankly, to revolt; it's time to just say, "No."

19 You may say, *"There just aren't enough Americans angry about this injustice, this servitude to government, this slavery.*

20 *"Americans are too comfortable, with their two television sets and two cars in the garage.*

21 *"They are not going to rise up angry and take their government back any time soon."*

22 You might be right.

23 But then again recall this: the patriot movement in 1776 was a minority cause; there were far more colonists who thought life under British tyranny was more than tolerable.

24 Being informed is the first step to achieving and maintaining freedom; only an educated and moral people can aspire to be free.

25 Some people are fighting back — instead of just protecting themselves by careful financial and tax planning — by actually challenging the government directly, in an effort to overturn the entire system; some Americans are challenging the IRS and the token 16th Amendment."

26 What's different about these statements?

27 Virtually everything else that is available on this subject is either one-sided activist argumentation, or establishment propaganda based on press releases by the IRS.

28 This ground breaking report is neither.

29 Perhaps not for the first time, here is an in-depth, critical, journalistic examination of the Income Tax, the 16th Amendment, the IRS and the legal strategies employed by those fighting "the system."

30 Much effort and research have gone into this report.

31 Your money — and life — are controlled by America's banking "system."

32 There is a reason for the deliberate dumbing down of America's public schools, the "drug war," and the persecution of Christians in the U.S., and more.

33 Perhaps Americans don't want to read these kinds of reports; they say they only want to be entertained; they say this is radical; they say it demands too much change; they say they don't care about what's right or wrong.

34 But they are wrong.

35 There is a growing resistance to tyranny by insurgents.

36 Reports like this one will not only help inform the American people, but will light the fuse of a new revolutionary spirit in this country — one that will help us to throw off our shackles and rekindle liberty's fire.

37 Why not strive to be free?

38 May the grace of our Lord Jesus Christ be with you all. Amen.

CHAPTER 2

THE federal government can implement whatever types of taxes it wants to implement **in its own territories**, under USC Article 1, Section 8, Clause 17.

2 This is called the "federal Zone" and it includes the District of Columbia, US territories and Possessions, and all federal enclaves within the states.

3 The Constitution says that all Direct Taxes must be apportioned to the states, according to USC Article 1, Section 9, Clause 4, and Article 1, Section 2, Clause 3.

4 Personal income taxes under Subtitle A of the IRC are constitutional and lawful *but apply only inside the "federal zone" and abroad, not within the states of the Union.*

5 "United States" = "District of Columbia". (*26 USC 7701 (a)(9) & (a)(10)*).

6 Collection may not lawfully be enforced *within the states of the Union* which are areas outside of the "federal zone".

7 There are no implementing regulations authorizing collection in the states of the Union.

8 The federal government has no legislative jurisdiction within the states of the Union, especially not with regard to legislation. (*Carter v. Carter Coal Co., 298 US 238 (1926)*).

9 Individual income taxes are not direct taxes, but indirect excise taxes upon a voluntary privilege called a "trade or business" which means a "public office" in the U.S. Government.

10 The only enforceable tax that public servants can assess, under the Internal Revenue Code (IRC), is *the profit of corporations domiciled in the district of Columbia* (the "federal zone").

11 Subtitle A of the IRC only apples to corporations and their officers domiciled in the District of Columbia who are the only "United States citizens" under the Internal Revenue Code. (*19 Corpus Juris Secundum, Section 886, a legal encyclopedia*).

12 A corporation is a "citizen" or "resident" of the state or country by or under the laws of which it was created, and of that state or country only.

13 The Supreme Court said that the meaning of "income" within the Internal Revenue Code means only "corporate profit". (*Bowers*

v. Kerbaugh-Empire Co., 271 US 170 (1926)).

14 The "income tax" is an indirect excise tax upon federally chartered corporations and corporate privileges.

15 The tax that most people think that they have to pay is a tax on an avoidable, privileged activity called a "trade or business" associated with the *federal corporation* called the United States government. (*28 USC 3002(15) (A)).*

16 The government can only tax that which it creates and the only thing it creates are *corporations.*

17 The government didn't create people so it can't tax people unless they individually volunteer to be taxed; this is the true meaning of the principle of "voluntary compliance" that the IRS uses.

18 The government doesn't want you to know this and therefore will not tell the truth in its publications about it.

19 The Supreme Court said that, *"Every man has a natural right to the fruits of his own labor; and no other person can rightfully deprive him of those fruits, and appropriate them against his will."* (*The Antelope, 23 US 66: (Wheat) (1825)).*

20 *"There is a clear distinction in this particular case between an individual and a corporation, and that the latter has no right to refuse to submit its books and papers for an examination at the suit of the State.*

21 *"The individual may stand upon his own way. His power to contract is unlimited. He owes no such duty to the State, since he receives nothing therefrom, beyond the protection of his life and property. His rights are such as existed by the law of the land long antecedent to the organization of the State, and can only be taken from him by due process of law, and in accordance with the Constitution.*

22 *Among his rights are a refusal to incriminate himself, and the immunity of himself and his property from arrest or seizure except under a warrant of the law. He owes nothing to the public so long as he does not trespass upon their rights."* (*Hale v. Henkel, 201 US 43 at 47 (1906)).*

23 May the grace of our Lord Jesus Christ be with you all. Amen.

CHAPTER 3

THE only legitimate purpose of taxes is to support the government and government employees on official business, not the people nor constituents.

2 *"tax: A charge by the government on the income of an individual, corporation, or trust, as well as the value of an estate or gift. The object of assessing the tax is to generate revenue to be used for the needs of the public.*

3 . . . *a pecuniary* (relating to money) *burden laid upon individuals or property to support the government, and is a payment exacted by legislative authority." In Mytinger, DC Tx. 31 F.Aupp. 977, 978, 979. "The essential characteristics of a tax are that it is NOT A VOLUNTARY PAYMENT OR DONATION, BUT AN ENFORCED CONTRIBUTION, EXACTED PURSUANT TO LEGISLATIVE AUTHORITY." Michigan Employment Sec. Commission v. Patt., 4 Mich. App. 228, 144 N.W.2d 663, 665. (Blacks Law Dictionary, 6th Edition, page 1457).*

4 *"A tax, in the general understanding of the term, and as used in the Constitution, signifies an exaction for the support of the government. The word has never been thought to connote the expropriation of money from one group for the benefit of another." (US v. Butler, 297 US 1 (1939)).*

5 *"To lay, with one hand, the power of the government on the property of the citizen, and with the other to bestow it upon favored individuals to aid private enterprises and build up private fortunes, is none the less a robbery because it is done under the forms of law and is called taxation. This is not legislation, it is a decree under legislative form.*

6 . . . *Nor is it taxation. 'A tax,' says Webster's Dictionary, 'is a rate or sum of money assessed on the person or property of a citizen by government for the use of the nation or State. Taxes are burdens of charges imposed by the Legislature upon persons or property to raise money for public purposes'." (Loan Association v. Topeka, 20 Wall. 655 (1874)).*

7 The government has attempted to satisfy the above Constitutional Supreme Court re-

quirement that the only people it can pay money to are federal employees and contractors by ensuring . . .

8 . . . that all "taxpayers" are public "officers" and federal "employees". . .

9 . . . that you must be a "taxpayer" in order to receive federal payments.

10 The IRS Form W-4 says "Employee Withholding Allowance Certificate". "Employee" is defined in 26 USC 3401(c) and 26 CFR § 31.3401(c)-1.

11 All "gross income" under Subtitle A must be "effectively connected with a trade or business" in the federal zone. 26 USC 871(a) is the only exception, and this income must also originate from within the federal zone.

12 "Income" earned outside of the federal zone is not taxable. (*26 USC 911(a)*).

13 The only "persons" against whom income tax may be enforced are identified in 26 USC 6671(b) and 26 USC 7343 as *"officers and employees of a corporation"* and the "corporation" they are talking about is defined in 28 USC 3002(15)(A) as *the corporate United States government.*

14 26 USC 6331(a) says that the only parties against whom distraint/enforcement can be implemented are elected or appointed officers of the federal government or a federal territory.

15 When you point out this fraud to the IRS, they try do dodge it by violating due process of law, using deceptive definitions, or the word "includes" to stretch definitions so that they have the excuse of "plausible deniability".

16 You can't earn self-employment income unless you are engaged in a "trade of business." (*26 USC 1402*).

17 The terms "married individual" and "single individual" are defined in 26 CFR 1.1-1(a)(2)(ii) as *"aliens with income effectively connected with a trade or business."* (a public office).

18 The Supreme Court has said that a man may not be compelled to use his property to benefit or help his fellow man.

19 *"Men are endowed by their Creator with certain unalienable rights, - 'life, liberty, and the pursuit of happiness' - and to 'secure', not grant or create,*

these rights governments are instituted. That property which a man has honestly acquired, he retains full control of, subject to these limitations: First, that he shall not use it to his neighbor's injury, and that does not mean that he must use it for his neighbor's benefit; second, that if he devotes it to a public use, he gives to the public a right to control that use: and third, that whenever the public needs require, the public may take it upon payment of due compensation." (Budd v. People of State of New York, 143 US 517 (1892)).

20 Why did the Supreme Court say this?

21 In a truly free country, people cannot be compelled to pay for government services or for "protection" that they do not want. To conclude otherwise is to sanction actions by the government to DESTROY self-government of the people over their own lives.

22 The only legitimate function of either law or government is "protection".

23 A taking of property without the consent of the person who is the object of the taking is "theft" in violation of the Ten Commandments.

24 Stealing a man's property or money under the "color of law" cannot be classified as "protection"; it is a crime in violation of 42 USC §1983 if anyone working for the government does it; let the doer beware.

25 Any government expense that funds any kind of charity or social program or wealth transfer cannot be paid for with an enforced contribution to the government called a "tax".

26 Any time the government gets into the charity or social welfare business, it is involved in "social insurance" and NOT "taxation" or a legitimate government function.

27 All "insurance" programs are voluntary and cannot legally be called "taxes", nor can payment be enforced with the authority of the law.

28 *"When the United States enters into commercial business it abandons its sovereign capacity and is to be treated like any other corporation." (91 Corpus Juris Secundom, United § 4).*

29 Can a private business force people to use and pay for its products and services? NO!

30 In the context of "social insurance", our government has created a private monopoly and abused its power to legislate to enforce participation in it and payment for its services.

31 Gigantic national monopolies of this kind are ILLEGAL under the Sherman Antitrust Act.

32 Any organization that compels participation and harms and persecutes those who don't participate is called a "protection racket" in violation of 18 USC 1951; organized crime.

33 Our federal government is involved in *organized crime* and *racketeering* if it deceives the public by identifying contributions which pay for "social insurance" as so called "taxes" whose payment can be enforced under the "color" but not under the "authority" of law.

34 . . . if it enforces payment for or participation in social programs.

35 . . . if it insists that payment for social insurance is "contractual" or mandatory but refuses to make the benefits equally contractual.

36 Compelled charity enforced by the government is nothing but slavery disguised as government benevolence, in violation of the 13th Amendment prohibition against slavery and involuntary servitude.

37 The Supreme Court has already said that Social Security is NOT a trust fund, is not contractual, and that the government has NO OBLIGATION to pay you anything. If the benefits aren't contractual, then payment for them CANNOT be either. (*Fleming v. Nestor, 363 US 603 (1960)*).

38 God gave churches and families EXCLUSIVE jurisdiction over charity and grace, and the above types of legal conflicts are the reason why He did this.

39 A failure or unwillingness by any church or pastor to recognize this legal and Constitutional reality is the biblical equivalent . . .

40 . . . of a violation of the First Commandment of love and trust and to obey God and His commandments with all our heart, soul, and mind.

41 . . . of government idolatry. The Book of Judges describes what happens to those who practice government idolatry. Gov-

ernment has become the new "god" and "religion" because it is filling the role that only churches can or should fill under God's laws.

42 . . . of surrender of church sovereignty to the government.

43 . . . of abdication of responsibility by pastors of the biblical and historical role of churches in society.

44 . . . of a diversion of the tithe away from its biblical role as a means for charity within churches, — to be used for personal vanity and gain.

45 May the grace of our Lord Jesus Christ be with you all. Amen.

CHAPTER 4

ONE doesn't pay individual income taxes to the IRS. Medicare, Welfare, and Social Security (FICA = Federal Insurance Contributions Act) are **not** taxes. They are government insurance programs. And all insurance programs are voluntary.

2 The government calls these programs "taxes" because they want to deceive you into thinking that paying them is a mandatory aspect of good citizenship.

3 The only people required to pay these "insurance premiums" are "aliens" of the United States of America.

4 Citizens of the United States of America are not the subject of the Internal Revenue Code.

5 Here is the definition of "individual" that applies to the government's 1040 Form, which is called "US Individual Income Tax Return":

6 26 CFR 1.1221-1: (c) Definitions, (3) individual, (i) alien individual.

7 The term "alien individual" means an individual who is not a "citizen" or "national" of the United States of America.

8 The United States is a corporate district within the United States of America.

9 When "taxes" are used for bribery and "wealth distribution" — instead of only supporting the government . . .

10 . . . then governments, judiciaries, and tax collection systems invariable become corrupt.

11 . . . then government invariably grows out of control because of the thirst for money and power.

12 . . . then the liberties of the people are eliminated one-by-one as taxes are increased and the tax code becomes a means of political control and tyranny.

13 Paying money to the IRS violates Man's Laws and is idolatry.

14 At least 56% of federal revenue is presently spent on wealth-transfer and social programs.

15 Since this is NOT authorized by the Constitution, according to the Supreme Court, the government is involved in theft and organized crime.

16 Remember? *"To lay, with one hand, the power of the government on the property of the citizen, and with the other to bestow it upon favored individuals to aid private enterprises and*

build up private fortunes, is none the less a robbery because it is done under the forms of law and is called taxation. This is not legislation, it is a decree under legislative forms.

17 . . . *Nor is it taxation. 'A tax,' says Webster's Dictionary, 'is a rate or sum of money assessed on the person or property of a citizen by government for the use of the nation or State. Taxes are burdens of charges imposed by the Legislature upon persons or property to raise money for public purposes'."* (*Loan Association v. Topeka, 20 Wall. 655 (1874)*).

18 The use of "taxes" for "wealth redistribution" violates Man's laws against Treason (*18 USC 2381*), Conflict of interest (*18 USC 208*), Expenditures to influence voting (*18 USC 597*), Robbery (*18 USC 2111*), Extortion (*18 USC 872*), Mailing threatening communications (*18 USC 873*), Blackmail (*18 USC 2381*), Peonage and slavery (*18 USC 1581; 42 USC 1994*), and slavery (*13th Amendment*).

19 It is fraud to call what one pays to the IRS a "tax"; it is instead a "donation" or "insurance premium" disguised as a "tax" to make it look mandatory.

20 *"Donatio: A gift. A transfer of the title of property to one who receives it without paying for it. The act by which the owner of a thing voluntarily transfers the title and possession of the same from himself to another person, without any consideration." (Blacks Law Dictionary, 6th Edition, page 487).*

21 *"Voluntary: Unconstrained by interference; unimpelled by another's influence; spontaneous; acting of oneself. Coker v. State, 199 Ga. 20, 33 S.E.2d 171, 174. Done by design or intention. Proceeding from the free and unrestrained will of the person. Produced in or by an act of choice. Resulting from the free and unrestrained will of the person. Produced in or by an act of choice. Resulting from free choice, without compulsion or solicitation. The word especially in statutes, often implies knowledge of essential facts. Without valuable consideration: as a voluntary deed." (Blacks Law Dictionary, 6th Edition, page 1474).*

22 The IRS doesn't maintain "tax record" about you, they maintain records of your "donations" if you live in a state of the Union, because in a state of the Union outside the federal zone you aren't subject to federal jurisdiction.

23 The federal income tax system under Subtitle A of the Internal Revenue Code is a "donation" program for the municipal government of the District of Columbia; i.e., the District United States; i.e., the "federal zone".

24 May the grace of our Lord Jesus Christ be with you all. Amen.

CHAPTER 5

WHO are taxpayers according to man's law?

2 The term "taxpayer," as defined in 26 USC § 7701(a)(14), means any person *subject* to any internal revenue tax.

3 "Taxpayers" consist of the following "persons" domiciled within the "federal zone" who have income connected with a public office in the United States Government called a "business" or "trade":

4 . . . non resident aliens with income connected to a public office in the US Government. (26 USC 1441).

5 . . . foreign Corporations. (26 USC 1442).

6 . . . foreign tax-exempt organizations. (26 USC 1443).

7 The term "subjected to" means *"Liable, subordinate, subservient, inferior, obedient to; governed or affected by; answerable for. Homan v. Employers Reinsurance Corp., 345 Mo. 650, 136 S.W.2d 289, 302."* (*Blacks Law, 6th Edition, page 1425*).

8 Federal courts are not allowed to determine if you are a "taxpayer". (*CIR v. Trustees of L. Inv. Ass'n, 100 F.2d 18 (1939)*).

9 Subtitle A of the Internal Revenue Code makes only withholding agents of nonresidential aliens "liable" in 26 USC § 1461.

10 No one else is "liable" unless they volunteer.

11 How does one volunteer? By just filling out a tax return and sending it in!

12 May the grace of our Lord Jesus Christ be with you all. Amen.

CHAPTER 6

R ENDER *unto Caesar the things that are Caesar's and unto God the things that are God's"* (*Mark 12:14-17, Bible, NKJV*).

2 Who is "Caesar" in America?

3 Americans don't have a Caesar or a King. in the literal sense, *per se.*

4 Who does the Constitution say are the "governing authorities"?

5 Do the government schools teach the ACCURATE answer to this vital question? And if not, why not?

6 *"This Constitution, and the laws of the United States which shall be made in pursuance thereof; and all treaties made, or which shall be made, under the Authority of the United States, shall be the supreme law of the land; and the Judges in every State shall be bound thereby, any thing in the constitution or laws of any State to the contrary notwithstanding."* (*US Constitution, Article VI, Clause 2*).

7 The reason the Constitution is the "Supreme Law of the land" is because the People wrote it; it is *delegated order* from the Master, who is represented by the People, to their *servants* in government.

8 According to Jesus, and natural law, the servant cannot be greater than the master.

9 *"No legislative act contrary to the Constitution can be valid. To deny this would be to affirm that the deputy (agent) is greater than his principal; that the servant is above the master; that the representatives of the people are superior to the people; that men, acting by virtue of powers may do not only what their powers do not authorize, but what they forbid. It is not otherwise to be supposed that the Constitution could intend to enable the representatives of the people to substitute their will to that of their constituents. It is far more rational to suppose, that the courts were designed to be an intermediate body between the people and the legislature, in order, among other things, to keep the latter within the province of the courts. A constitution is, in fact, and must be regarded by judges, as fundamental law. If there should happen to be an irreconcilable variance*

between the two, the Constitution is to be preferred to the statute." (*Alexander Hamilton, Federalist paper # 78*).

10 Caesar demanded a Constitution to limit government power and thereby preserve maximum liberty for all, but more especially for himself.

11 *"The history of liberty is the history of the limitation of governmental power, not the increase of it."* (*Woodrow Wilson, President of the United States*).

12 *"The glory of our American system of government is that it was created by a written Constitution which protects the people against the exercise of arbitrary, unlimited power, and the limits of which instrument may not be passed by the government it created, or by any branch of it, or even by the people who ordained it, except by amendment or change of its provisions."* (*Downes v. Bidwell, 182 US 244; 21 S.Ct. 770 (1901)*).

13 How did the Constitution limit government power?

14 . . . by separating powers to prevent them from concentrating in one party, group, or office.

15 . . . by breaking the federal government into three separate branches: Executive, Legislative, and Judicial.

16 . . . by leaving all powers not delegated to the federal government with the People and the States in the 10th Amendment.

17 Here is who the US Supreme Court said the "governing authorities" are in America.

18 *"The rights of individuals and the justice due to them, are as dear and precious as those of states. Indeed the latter are founded upon the former; and the great end and object of them must be to secure and support the rights of individuals, or else vain is government."* (*Chisholm v. Georgia, 2 US (2 Dall.) 419, 1 L.Ed 440 (1793)*).

19 *"A State does not owe its origin to the government of the United States, in the highest or in any of its branches. It was in existence before it. It derives its authority from the same pure and sacred source as itself; the voluntary and deliberate choice of the people. A State is altogether exempt from the jurisdiction of the Courts of the United States, or from any other exte-*

rior authority, unless in the special instances when the general Government has power derived from the Constitution itself." (*Ibid*).

20 "*Sovereignty itself is, of course, not subject to law, for it is the author and source of law. While sovereign powers are delegated to the government, sovereignty itself remains with the people,*" (*Yick Wo v. Hopkins, 118 US 356 (1886)*).

21 "*The ultimate authority ... resides in the people alone.* (*James Madison, The Federalists, No. 46*).

22 "*The words 'people of the United States' and 'citizens,' are synonymous terms and mean the same thing. They both describe the political body who, according to our republican institutions, form the sovereignty, and who hold the power* (of sovereignty) *and conduct the government* (govern themselves) *through their representatives. They are what we familiarly call the 'sovereign people,' and every citizen is one of this people, and a constituent member of this sovereignty.*" (*Boyd v. State of Nebraska, 143 US 135*

(1892)).

23 "*In the United States, sovereignty resides in the people ... the Congress cannot invoke the sovereign power of the People to override their will as thus declared.*" (*Perry v. US, 294 US 330 (1935)*).

24 "*Governments are but trustees acting under derived authority and have no power to delegate what is not delegated to them. But the people, as the original fountain might take away what they have delegated and intrust to whom they please. The sovereignty in every state resides in the people of the state and they may alter and change their form of government at their own pleasure.*" (*Luther v. Borden, 48 US 1, 12 LED 581 (1849)*).

25 "*There is no such thing as a power of inherent sovereignty in the government of the United States. In this country sovereignty resides in the people, and congress can exercise no power which they have not, by their Constitution entrusted to it: All else is withheld.*" (*Julliard v. Greenman, 110 US 421 (1884)*).

26 "*In the United States, sov-*

ereignty resides in the people who act through the organs established by the Constitution. The Congress as the instrumentality of sovereignty is endowed with certain powers to be exerted on behalf of the people in the manner and with the effect the Constitution ordains. The Congress cannot invoke the sovereign power of the people to override their will as thus declared." (Perry v. United States, 294 US 330, 353 (1915)).

27 Your government and the Constitution both say that YOU are "Caesar"!

28 Your public servants are NOT "Caesar"; they are your SERVANTS.

29 *"Servants, be submissive to your masters with all fear, not only to the good and gentle, but also to the harsh. For this is commendable, if because of conscience toward God one endures grief, suffering wrongfully." (1 Peter 2:18-19, Bible, NKJV).*

30 This arrangement is unique in all the world. No other country does it this way.

31 *"From the differences existing between feudal sovereignties and Government founded on* compacts, it necessarily follows that their respective prerogatives must differ. Sovereignty is the right to govern; a nation or State-sovereign is the person or persons in whom that resides. In Europe the sovereignty is generally ascribed to the Prince; here in America it rests with the people; there, the sovereign actually administers the Government; here in America never a single instance; our Governors are the agents of the people, and at most stand in the same relation to their sovereign, in which regents in Europe stand to their sovereigns. Their Princes have personal powers, dignities, and pre-eminences, our rulers have none but official; nor do they partake in the sovereignty otherwise, or in any other capacity, than as private citizens." (Chisholm, Ex'r. v. Georgia, 2 Dall. (US) 499, 1 L.ed. 454, 457, 471, 472 (1794)).*

32 Citizenship in America is a STEWARDSHIP that God gave us over our servants in government.

33 *"The people of this State, as the successors of its former sovereign, are entitled to all the*

right which formerly belonged to the King by his prerogative. Through the medium of their Legislature they may exercise all the powers which previous to the Revolution could have been exercised whether by the King alone, or by him in conjunction with the Parliament; subject only to those restrictions which have been imposed by the Constitution of this State or the United States." (Lansing v. Smith, 21 D. 89. 4 Wendel 9 (1829) (New York)).

34 America is the "Land of Kings". The Constitution makes YOU the "king"; not your "public servants".

35 What are YOU doing with this sacred Stewardship?

36 May the grace of our Lord Jesus Christ be with you all. Amen.

CHAPTER 7

THE Bible establishes the fact that the Creator is the owner of all things.

2 In other words, the creator of a thing is the owner of the thing.

3 *"The heavens are Yours* (God's), *the earth also is Yours: the world and all its fullness, You have founded them."* (*Psalm 89:11-12, Bible, NKJV*).

4 The owner can do whatever he wants with his creation.

5 *"All the inhabitants of the earth are reputed as nothing; He does according to His will in the army of heaven And among the inhabitants of the earth. No one can restrain His hand Or say to Him, 'What have You done'?* (*Daniel 4:35, Bible, NKJV*).

6 The created cannot be greater than its creator.

7 *"Woe to him who strives with his Maker! Let the potsherd strive with the potsherds of the earth! Shall the clay say to him who forms it, 'What are you making?' Or shall your handiwork say, 'He has no hands?'' Woe to him who says to his father, 'What are you beginning?' Or to the woman, 'What have you brought forth?'"* (*Isaiah 45:9-10, Bible, NKJV*).

8 *"If the time shall ever arrive when, for an object appealing, however strongly, to our sympathies, the dignity of the States shall bow to the dictation of Congress by conforming their legislation thereto, when the power and majesty and honor of those who created* (the federal government) *shall become subordinate to the thing of their creation, I but feebly utter my apprehensions when I express my firm conviction that we shall see 'the beginning of the end'."* (*Steward machine Co. v. Davis, 301 US 548 (1937)*).

9 We the People, as the Sovereigns, created government to be our SERVANT and protector. The Constitution is a finite delegator of authority to the SERVANTS:

10 *"That to secure these rights, governments are instituted among men, deriving their just powers from the CONSENT of the governed."* (*Declaration of Independence, 1776*).

11 *"Having thus avowed my disapprobation of the purposes, for which the terms, State and sovereign, are frequently used,*

and of the object, to which the application of the last of them is almost universally made; it is now proper that I should disclose the meaning, which I assign to both, and the application (US 419, 455), which I make of the latter. In doing this, I shall have occasion incidentally to evince, how true it is, that States and Governments were made for (and by) *man; and, at the same time, how true it is, that his creatures and servants have first deceived, next vilified, and, at last, oppressed their master and maker." (Justice Wilson, Chisholm v. Georgia, 2 Dall. (2 US) 419, 1 L.Ed 440, 455 (1793)).*

12 The Constitution created a government of limited, enumerated and delegated powers from the source of ALL power, the People.

13 Our "public servants" are "bondservants", and the "bond" is the Constitution.

14 - *5 Bondservants, be obedient to those who are your masters according to the flesh, with fear and trembling, in sincerity of heart, as to Christ; 6 not with eyeservice* (or political lip-service), *as men-pleasers, but as bond-servants of Christ, doing the will of God from the heart, 7 with goodwill doing service, as to the Lord, and not to men, 8 knowing that whatever good anyone does, he will receive the same from the Lord, whether he is a slave or free. 9 And you, masters, do the same things to them, giving up threatening, knowing that your own master also is in heaven, and there is no partiality with Him." (Ephesians 6:5-9, Bible, NKJV).*

15 Natural Order is based on the sequence by which things were created. This sequence, from the greatest to the least, is:

16 (1) God.

17 (2) Man, as individual, not as a collective.

18 The creations of man are: Families; Contracts; Trusts; Elections; Petit Juries; Organized churches.

19 (3) State constitutions.

20 The creations of the state governments authorized by the state constitutions are:

21 Independent branches of state governments, including Executive, Legislative, Judicial; State statutes; State regulations; State

corporations.

22 (4) The Federal Constitution.

23 The creations of the federal government are: Executive, legislative, Judicial; Federal statutes; Federal regulations; Federal corporations; Federal territories.

24 America has a "Republican Form of Government" mandated by Article 4, Section 4, of the Constitution . . . not a democracy;

25 . . . wherein the People hold all sovereign power, governing themselves through their SERVANTS—their elected representatives.

26 Jesus said that the servant cannot be greater than the master:

27 *"Most assuredly, I say to you, a servant is not greater than his master, nor is he who is sent greater than he who sent him." (Jesus, at John 13:16, Bible, NKJV).*

28 It is a sin to have an earthly King or "Caesar" over us as Christians.

29 - *6 But the thing displeased Samuel when they said, 'Give us a king to judge us.' So Samuel prayed to the Lord. 7 And the Lord said to Samuel, 'Heed the voice of the people in all that* *they say to you; for they have rejected Me, that I should not reign over them. 8 According to all the works which they have done since the day that I brought them up out of Egypt, even to this day—with which they have forsaken Me and served other gods—so they are doing to you also* (government becoming idolatry)." *(1 Samuel 8:6-8, Bible, NKJV).*

30 *"And all the people said to Samuel, 'Pray for your servants to the Lord your God, that we may not die; for we have added to all our sins the evil of asking a king for ourselves." (1 Samuel 12:19, Bible, NKJV).*

31 God is our only "Caesar", Lawgiver and King, as Christians.

32 *"Indeed they* (the governments and the men who make them up in relation to God) *are all worthless: their works are nothing; their molded images* (and their bureaus and agencies and usurious "codes" that are not law) *are wind* (and vanity) *and confusion." (Isaiah 41:29, Bible, NKJV).*

33 We cannot allow our SERVANTS in government to domi-

neer or disobey their master. Anyone who does, Congress labels as a COMMUNIST. (50 USC 841).

34 Our own apathy and indifference to politics has allowed the SERVANTS to domineer, resulting in the transformation of our "Republic" into a "Dulocracy".

35 *"Dulocracy: A government where servants and slaves have so much license and privilege that they domineer."* (*Blacks Law Dictionary, 6th Edition, page 501*).

36 What did God create?

37 *"For God is the King of all the earth; Sing praises with understanding."* (*Psalm 47:7, Bible, NKJV*).

38 *"Oh, let the nations be glad and sing for joy! For you* (God) *shall judge the people righteously, And govern* (ALL) *the nations on earth."* (*Psalm 67:4, Bible, NKJV*).

39 *"Arise, O God, judge the earth; For you* (God) *shall inherit all nations* (and governments of nations). *"* (*Psalm 82:8, Bible, NKJV*).

40 *"I have made the earth, And created man on it. I, My hands, stretched out the heavens, And all their host I have commended."* (*Isaiah 45:12, Bible, NKJV*).

41 *"The heavens are Yours* (God's), *the earth also is Yours; The world and all its fullness, You have founded them. The north and the south, You have created them; Tabor and Hermon rejoice in Your name. You have a mighty arm; Strong is Your hand, and high is Your right hand."* (*Psalm 89:11-13, Bible, NKJV*).

42 *"In the beginning God created the heavens and the earth."* (*Genesis 1:1, Bible, NKJV*).

43 *"Indeed heaven and the highest heavens belong to the Lord your God, also the earth with all that is in it."* (*Deut. 10:14, Bible, NKJV*).

44 *"Therefore let no one boast in men. For all things are yours* (not Caesar's); *whether Paul or Apollos or Cephas, or the world or life or death, or things present or things to come—all are yours. And you are Christ's, and Christ is God's."* (*1 Corinthians 3:21-13, Bible, NKJV*).

45 Question: If God created the Heavens and the Earth, and owns

them and everything else, then what is left that belongs to "Caesar"? What did "Caesar" create?

46 "Caesar"—the People individually here in America—used the Constitution to create and define a stewardship for their public servants.

47 The sole purpose of the stewardship is to secure our God-given equal rights as sovereign individuals under God.

48 *"We hold these truths to be self-evident, that all men are created equal, that they are endowed by their Creator with certain unalienable Rights, that among these are Life, Liberty and the pursuit of happiness.— That to secure these rights, Governments are instituted among Men." (Declaration of Independence, 1776).*

49 Securing our rights is the foundation of the second great commandment to love our neighbor as ourselves, as in Exodus 20:12-17. Securing and protecting rights is how we love our neighbor; how we respect our neighbor; and we honor God (the first of the two great commandments).

50 Securing our rights is done by enacting laws that punish and prevent sins which hurt others; and by delegating police powers to local governments and allowing them to enforce the laws to protect others.

51 May the grace of our Lord Jesus Christ be with you all. Amen.

CHAPTER 8

THE "governing authorities" are the People. And their un changing and immutable will is clearly expressed in the Constitution <u>for</u> the United States.

2 The Constitution does NOT allow the IRS to collect the kind of taxes that it collects within the states of the Union, as was earlier shown.

3 Government has been assigned the job to protect us all.

4 When we don't obey the law, government is deprived of the ability to protect our neighbor, and we violate the second commandment to love our neighbor.

5 - 1 Let every soul be subject to the governing authorities. For there is no authority except from God, and the authorities that exist are appointed by God. 2 Therefore whoever resists the authority resists the ordinance of God, and those who resist will bring judgment on themselves. 3 For rulers are not a terror to good works, but to evil. Do you want to be unafraid of the authority? Do what is good. But if you do evil, be afraid; 4 for he does not bear the sword in vain; for he is God's minis-ter, an avenger to execute wrath on him who practices evil. 5 Therefore you must be subject, not only because of wrath but also for conscience' sake. 6 For because of this you also pay taxes, for they are God's ministers attending continually to this very thing. 7 Render therefore to all their due: taxes to whom taxes are due, customs to whom customs, fear to whom fear, honor to whom honor." (*Romans 13:1-7, Bible, NKJV*).

6 May the grace of our Lord Jesus Christ be with you all. Amen.

CHAPTER 9

THE government needs funds in order to satisfy its mission: "to protect our neighbors from harm."

2 Our Founding Fathers knew that government needed money to satisfy its mission, and provided in the Constitution two ways for government to raise revenue: Direct taxation and Indirect taxation.

3 Direct taxes must be apportioned among the several states of the Union and can only be imposed as temporary, emergency wartime tax.

4 Indirect taxes are taxes imposed on a service or privilege such as engaging in a specific activity like purchasing property or goods.

5 Enforcement of any form of taxation that is not authorized by the Constitution essentially amounts to organized extortion by the government. We call such extortion "The Federal Mafia".

6 The Bible encourages believers to pay "taxes" that are LAWFULLY owed, but neither it nor enacted law allows the government to FORCE us . . .

7 . . . to subsidize wealth transfer (*theft in violation of the Ten Commandments*).

8 . . . to subsidize charity or welfare conducted by the government; this is the exclusive jurisdiction of the church and the family.

9 . . . to donate money to the government that no law requires them to pay.

10 . . . to facilitate or help those who are demanding money that the Constitution forbids them to collect; this would be aiding and abetting TREASON.

11 We must read and know what the Constitution and enacted law allows Congress to do in regards to taxation.

12 There is no enacted law requiring "natural persons" in states of the Union to pay anything to the IRS.

13 By "donating" money to the IRS we are . . .

14 . . . violating God's law;

15 . . . spreading socialism;

16 . . . and encouraging government dependencies, and oppression of our rights, liberties and privacy by the government.

17 May the grace of our Lord Jesus Christ be with you all. Amen.

CHAPTER 10

P AYING money to the IRS violates God's laws.

2 God's laws are violated when taxation is used for wealth redistribution.

3 - 10 *My son, If sinners* (socialists, in this case) *entice you, Do not consent. 11 If they say, 'Come with us, Let us lie in wait to shed blood* (of innocent "non-taxpayers"); *Let us lurk secretly for the innocent without cause; 12 Let us swallow them alive like Sheol, And whole, like those who go down to the Pit: 13 We shall fill our houses with spoil* (plunder); *14 Cast in your lot among us, Let us all have one purse* (share the redistributed stolen LOOT) — *15 My son, do not walk in the way with them* (do not ASSOCIATE with them and don't let the government FORCE you to associate with them either by forcing you to become a "taxpayer" or a "US citizen"). *Keep your foot from their path; 16 For their feet run to evil, and they make haste to shed blood. 17 Surely, in vain the net is spread in the sight of any bird; 18 But they lie in wait for their own lives. 19 So are the ways of everyone who is greedy for gain* (or unearned government benefits); *It takes away the life of its owners."* (*Proverbs 1:10-19*).

4 Paying money to the government that is used for wealth redistribution is idolatry and Socialism — men cannot have more power over you than God.

5 Christians cannot be socialists.

6 *"In the name of the Lord Jesus Christ, we command you brothers, to keep away from every brother who is idle and does not live according to the teaching you received from us."* (*2 Thessalonians 3:6, Bible, NIV*).

7 How can we "keep away" from idle brothers if the Feds force us to SUPPORT them?

8 We cannot subsidize a government program that condones idleness and dependency and which does not hold men responsible for supporting themselves or living a moral life style. These fundamental defects pervade every single government program to help the *so-called* "needy".

9 May the grace of our Lord Jesus Christ be with you all. Amen.

CHAPTER 11

E VEN the US Supreme Court confirms that the authority of law cannot be used to compel a person to help his neighbor.

2 *"Surely the matters in which the public has the most interest are the supplies of food and clothing; yet can it be that by reason of this interest the state may fix the price at which the butcher must sell his meat, or the vendor of boots and shoes his goods? Men are endowed by their Creator with certain unalienable rights, - 'life, liberty, and the pursuit of happiness' - and to 'secure', not grant or create, these rights governments are instituted. That property which a man has honestly acquired, he retains full control of, subject to these limitations: First, that he shall not use it to his neighbor's injury, and that does not mean that he must use it for his neighbor's benefit; second, that if he devotes it to a public use, he gives to the public a right to control that use: and third, that whenever the public needs require, the public may take it upon payment of due compensation." (Budd v. People of State of New York, 143 US 517 (1892)).*

3 The government has no jurisdiction over charity or grace. These are the exclusive provinces of the family and the church under God's law, and they are to be implemented through church tithes and family giving, and NOT through government programs.

4 Compelling our neighbor to surrender his property to help his neighbor is NOT charity, but theft and slavery disguised as government benevolence.

5 *"Thou shalt not steal."* (*Exodus 20:15, Bible, NKJV*).

6 *"And if one of your brethren who dwells by you becomes poor* (or lazy, or apathetic, or irresponsible), *and sells himself to you, you shall not compel him to serve as a* (government) *slave* (by forcing him to participate in income taxes). " (*Leviticus 25:39, Bible, NKJV*).

7 Our neighbor must consent to help his neighbor or we are enslaving him.

8 *"Stand fast therefore in the liberty by which Christ has made us free, and do not be entangled again with a yoke of*

bondage (or slavery to the government, the legal profession, or the income tax)." (*Galatians 5:1, Bible, NKJV*).

9 Being compelled to pay money that no law or Constitution requires one to pay amounts to a compelled bribe to a government official.

10 It is *illegal* to use money to bribe public officials. (18 USC § 210).

11 It is *illegal* to use these donations to bribe voters with social handouts. (18 USC § 597).

12 It is *illegal* for a judge to rule on a tax issue if he pays income taxes or accepts benefits derived from income taxes, himself. (28 USC 144, 29 USC 455).

13 *"The king establishes the land by justice; but he who receives* (compelled) *bribes* (extortion under color of law) *overthrows it."* (*Proverb 29:4, Bible, NKJV*).

14 Charity and free will must coexist; Christians who love their neighbor cannot force or compel them to do anything but stop hurting others.

15 We cannot associate with or especially subsidize a government that is competing with churches for jurisdiction over welfare and charity.

16 *"Come out from among them* (the unbelievers) *and be separate, says the Lord. Do not touch what is unclean, and I will receive you. I will be a Father to you, and you shall be my sons and daughters, says the Lord Almighty."* (*2 Corinthians 6:17-18. Bible, NKJV*).

17 When Jesus paid us his last visit, he came to call sinners to repentance. (Mark 2:17).

18 The first sinners Jesus met with were "Tax collators". (Matthew 9:11).

19 The phrase "tax collectors" nearly always appears together with the word "sinners" throughout the New Testament.

20 *"For God gives wisdom and knowledge* (and education) *and joy to a man who is good in His sight; but to the sinner He gives the work of gathering and collecting* (unlawfully stealing, in this case). *This also is vanity and grasping for the wind."* (*Eccles. 2:26, Bible, NKJV*)

21 *"Then tax collectors came to be baptized, and said to him* (to John the Baptizer) *'Teacher* (educator) *what shall we do* (to

be saved)*?' And he said to them, 'Collect no more than what is appointed to you* (under the law)*'." (Luke 3:12-13, Bible, NKJV).*

22 We can't love God and at the same time *subsidize* the evil described here without being detestable hypocrites.

23 The love of money is the root of all evil, according to John in *1 Timothy 6:10.*

24 How our government handles and uses and collects our money is the first and most important place where virtue is necessary.

25 Money and how it is handled, in fact, is the barometer of any society's virtue.

26 Deceit in commerce is the sin MOST detested by the Lord, and "tribute" is a form of commerce.

27 As religion towards God is a branch of universal righteousness, righteousness towards men is a branch of true religion, for he is not a godly man who is not honest, nor can he expect that his devotions would be accepted; for nothing is more offensive to God than deceit in commerce.

28 A false balance is a type of all manner of unjust and fraudulent practices in dealing with any person; it is an affront to justice as well as a wrong to our neighbor, of whom God is the protector.

29 Men make light of such frauds, and think that there is no sin in that in which there is money to be had, and as such pass undiscovered, they do not blame themselves.

30 But commercial sins are none the less an abomination to God, who will be the avenger for those who are defrauded by their brethren.

31 Nothing is more pleasing to God than fair and honest dealing, nor more necessary to make us and our devotions acceptable to him; a just weight is His delight.

31 A false balance cheats, whether it be in the federal courtroom or at the IRS, or in the marketplace under the pretence of doing right which is the greater abomination to God.

32 May the grace of our Lord Jesus Christ be with you all. Amen.

CHAPTER 12

THE power to tax is the power to destroy. And to take away the property rights that the people possess. So the Founding Fathers designed the Constitution to prevent such tyrannical events.

2 There are only two types of taxes allowed — direct taxes and indirect taxes — established on this rule of thumb:

3 No direct taxes are to be charged directly to the people — unless voluntarily paid.

4 Only indirect taxes can be charged directly to the people — such as sales taxes, or excise taxes on privileges, applied for and exercised.

5 The Founding Fathers limited the power of government per the teachings of Jesus.

4 The charge against Jesus included his telling others NOT to pay taxes to Caesar.

5 *"And they began to accuse* (Jesus)*, saying, We found this fellow perverting the nation, and forbidding to give tribute to Caesar, saying that he himself is Christ a King."* (*Luke 23:2, Bible KJV*).

6 - 24 *And when they had come to Capernaum, they that received tribute money came to Peter, and saith, Doth not your master pay tribute? 25 He saith, Yes."* (Peter misunderstood Jesus' teachings on this vital point). *And when he was come into the house, Jesus prevented* (corrected) *him, saying, What thinkest thou, Simon? of whom do the kings of the earth take custom or tribute? of their own children, or of strangers? 26 Peter saith unto him, Of strangers. Jesus saith unto him, Then are the children free."* (tax exempt.) *27 Notwithstanding, lest we should offend them* (the tax collectors)*, go thou to the sea, and cast an hook, and take up the fish that first cometh up; and when thou hast opened his mouth, thou shalt find a piece of money; that take, and give unto them for me and thee.* (*Matthew 17:24-27, Bible, NKJV*).

7 Jesus conceded as a *"suffer it to be so now"* accommodation to the tax collectors and Peter. He did not order his purse keeper Judas to pay a tax from the disciple's purse.

8 Look at IRS Form W-7, used

to obtain a "taxpayer ID number."

9 There are only three types of W-7 forms, and none apply to domestic Americans.

11 Personal taxes (direct taxes) are to be taken only from *"U.S. citizens abroad and aliens at home";* all other personal taxes are voluntary contributions to the IRS. *(See 26 CFR § 1.1-1(a)(2)(ii) and 26 CFR § 301, 6109-1(d)(3))*.

12 Citizens of the Republic *(non U.S. citizens)* are "sovereign nationals" and "nonresident aliens", according to the IRS — they are *sovereign* over their own person and labor (e.g., having SOVEREIGN IMMUNITY).

13 Jesus said that the "kings of the earth" are to only tax "strangers", that are "aliens" of the Republic under the IRC. It is the purpose of the government of the Republic to protect its "citizens".

14 Any government or official that has the authority to use the force of law to steal from its citizens has a conflict of interest in violation of 18 USC 208: "Acts affecting a personal financial interest".

15 Judges who are "taxpayers" and "citizens" can be and often are threatened and harassed by the IRS if they rule against the IRS.

16 It is impossible to have a fair trial against a "citizen" who refuses to volunteer to pay taxes to the government if every one who could be selected from the jury pool is a taxpayer and more importantly a tax consumer; all the jurists would have a conflict of interest under 18 USC 597.

17 No retired jurist receiving a socialist handout would ever let a fellow citizen reduce their benefits by refusing to volunteer to participate in the tax system.

18 Those who are already voluntarily paying will envy those who aren't and take sides against them; the government abuses this tactic all the time in tax trials.

19 May the grace of our Lord Jesus Christ be with you all. Amen.

CHAPTER 13

W HAT should we render to Caesar?

2 Answer: What the delegated Orders to our public servants (*the Constitution*) says we should render unto Caesar.

3 Taxes on profits connected with imports into the Republic ONLY; other types of taxes are legitimate only on activities within the District of Columbia under IRC Subtitle A.

4 To state governments, every tax that does not depend upon federal liability, but most state income taxes assume that the payer is domiciled on federal property, which most people in the states are not.

5 What does the Bible say should be "Rendered unto Caesar?

6 *"Render to Caesar that which is Caesar's" (Mark 12:14-17, Bible, NKJV).*

7 That which is Caesar's is that which he creates.

8 - 6 *"Render to her* ("Babylon the Great Harlot": an atheist totalitarian democracy) *just as she rendered to you, and repay her double according to her works; in the cup which she*

has mixed, mix double for her.

7 *"In the measure that she glorified herself and lived luxuriously, in the same measure give her torment and sorrow; for she says in her heart, 'I sit as queen, and am no widow, and will not see sorrow.' 8 "Therefore her plagues will come in one day— death and morning and famine. And she will be utterly burned with fire, for strong is the Lord God who judges her. (Revelation 18:6-8, Bible, NKJV).*

9 The only thing Caesar creates is paper *money substitutes,* privileged *federal employment,* and privileged *federal corporations.*

10 People are attracted to corporations because of limited liability.

11 Corporate income taxes amount to only "liability insurance".

12 Limited liability encourages sin without consequences.

13 Limited liability encourages men to hurt their neighbor, and thereby violate the *second* of the two great commandments: *to love our neighbor.*

14 God emphasizes personal responsibility in His word rather

than limited liability.

15 The Bible says that "trusting in privileges" — whether in the form of limited liability or other means — is a characteristic of hypocrites and violates His sacred precept of "equal protection" for all.

16 Jesus vehemently criticized and hated hypocrites.

17 Limited liability economies are socialistic, and bestow totalitarian authority to governments that are a threat to liberty.

18 A limited liability economy is socialistic.

19 By seeking to protect people, a limited liability economy simply transfers responsibility away from the people to the state, where central "government planning" obviates personal responsibility.

20 Limited liability encourages people to take chances with limited risks — and to sin economically without paying the price.

21 Limited liability laws rest on the fallacy that payment for economic sins need not be made.

22 In actuality, payment liability is transferred to others.

32 Limited liability laws were unpopular in earlier Christian eras but flourish in the Darwinian world.

33 Limited liability laws rest upon important religious presuppositions.

34 Federal Reserve Notes (FRNs) have no intrinsic worth at all — Federal Reserve Notes are not money.

35 *"Money, in usual and ordinary acceptation, means coins and paper currency used as a circulating medium of exchange, and does not embrace notes* (Federal Reserve Notes), *bonds, evidences of debt, or other personal or real estate. Lane v. Railey, 280 Ky. 319 S.W.2d 74, 79, 81."* (*Black's Law Dictionary, 6th Edition, page 1005*).

36 The value of Federal Reserve Notes is regulated by the money supply.

37 Federal Reserve Notes are corporate bond/debt instruments, where the corporation is the for profit corporate United States.

38 The main method for regulating the supply is the income tax, which is usurious, dishonest, unjust.

39 The income tax makes you into surety for the debts of irre-

sponsible politicians; Revelation 19:19 calls these politicians "The Beast".

40 The income tax makes you surety to guarantee the value of the currency.

41 The income tax encourages irresponsibility and debt by our politicians; the Bible says that we can't borrow debt as a nation: Deut. 15:6; Deut. 28:12; Deut. 23:19-20.

42 The income tax subsidizes a private, for profit corporate monopoly called the Federal Reserve.

43 Tax money cannot be used for the benefit of anyone but the general public, without violating the Constitution.

44 Those who carry or use Federal Reserve Notes are therefore "surety for the debts of a stranger" — our sinful government.

45 *"A man devoid of understanding shakes hands in a pledge* (income tax return), *and becomes surety for his friend."* (*Proverbs 17:18, Bible, NKJV*).

46 *"He who is surety for a* (government politician) *stranger will suffer, but one who hates being surety is secure."* (*Proverb*

11:15, Bible NKJV).

47 - 1 *"My son, if you become surety for your friend* (and especially a politician), *if you have shaken hands in pledge for a stranger, 2 you are snared by the words of your mouth; you are taken by the words of your mouth. 3 So do this, my son, and deliver yourself; for you have come into the hand of your friend* (your slaver): *Go and humble yourself; plead with your friend. 4 Give no sleep to your eyes, nor slumber to your eyelids. 5 Deliver yourself like a gazelle from the hand of the hunter; and like a bird from the hand of the fowler."* (*Proverb 6:1-5, Bible NKJV*).

48 If we interpret God's commands in the Bible literally, we must conclude that :

49 The government can only spend the tax money we give it to protect us, not for social welfare.

50 Social welfare is the exclusive jurisdiction of churches and families.

51 The original function of the tithe was a means of social welfare to support the church; and the tithe is never more than 10%.

52 Since the government didn't create the land or the people, it can't lawfully tax either one.

53 Direct property taxes and direct personal taxes are antibiblical, unconstitutional, and not natural.

54 *"The earth is the Lord's, and the fullness thereof"*.

55 A tax on the land is a tax against God and the order of His law.

56 God Himself does not tax the land which He gives to men as a stewardship under Him;

57 The only legitimate tax is God's tax on His follower's increase—the tithe.

58 The tithe is an "income tax" of 10% and no more.

59 Any giving beyond the tithe is an *offering of freewill.*

60 May the grace of our Lord Jesus Christ be with you all. Amen.

CHAPTER 14

IN the legal field, "Domicile" is equal to "Allegience."

2 "domicile" refers to a person's legal home; *that place where a man has his true, fixed, and permanent home and principal establishment, and to which whenever he is absent he has the intention of returning."* (*Smith v. Smith, 206 Pa.Super. 310m 213 A.2d 94*).

3 *"Generally, physical presence within a state and the intention to make it one's home are the requisites of establishing a "domicile" therein . . .*

4 *"The permanent residence of a person or the place to which he intends to return even though he may actually reside elsewhere . . .*

5 *"A person may have more than one residence but only one domicile . . .*

6 *"The legal domicile of a person is important since it — rather than the actual residence — often controls the jurisdiction of the taxing authorities and determines where a person may exercise the privilege of voting and other legal rights and privileges."* (*Black's Law Dictionary,*

6th Edition, page 485).

7 Domicile is a person's "legal home".

8 Domicile is the source of "the law" and "permanent protection" that a person claims allegiance to.

9 Domicile is based on the coincidence of "intent" to live somewhere, NOT on where a person actually physically lives.

10 Only the person can define and express his "intent".

11 Government cannot coerce a person to declare places within its jurisdiction as his "domicile".

12 For Christians, the Lord is the source of all of our permanent protection and we may not rely on man's law as a substitute or replacement for His protection.

13 The term "permanent" means a relationship of continuing, lasting nature as distinguished from temporary, but a relationship may be permanent even though it is one that may be dissolved eventually at the instance either of the United States or of the individual, in accordance with law. (*8 USC § 1101(a) (31)*).

14 The only thing "permanent" in the Bible is God and Heaven.

15 The earth will be destroyed and remade (*Isaiah 66:22*), therefore we cannot literally make earth a "permanent place of abode" or "domicile" without committing idolatry.

16 Claiming our "domicile" to be anyplace but "heaven" as a Christian amounts to idolatry.

17 The most Christians can be here are "transient foreigners".

18 . . . not "inhabitants" who have an earthly domicile.

19 . . . not "residents" who have an earthly domicile.

20 You can't vote or serve on jury duty as a citizen without having a domicile within the government you are participating in.

21 A Christian is a "national", not a "citizen".

22 A person who is a "national" but not a "citizen" is treated as a "nonresident alien" of the U.S. under the Internal Revenue Code.

23 - 8 *Then Haman said to King Ahasuerus, 'There is a certain people* (Christians/Jews) *scattered and dispersed among the people in all the provinces of your kingdom; their laws are different from all other people's, and they do not keep the king's laws.* 9 *'Therefore it is not fit-*

ting for the king to let them remain. If it pleases the king, let a decree be written that they be destroyed, and I will pay ten thousand talents of silver into the hands of those who do the work, to bring it into the king's treasuries." (*Esther 3:8-9, Bible, NKJV*).

24 In this Scripture, the Jews were criticized by the government because they did not claim the King's land for their "domicile" and thereby participate in his corrupt system of "tribute/taxation" because they did not want to commit idolatry.

25 One's "domicile" establishes the "situs" or place where paying "tribute" may be enforced under the authority of law.

26 *"situs: Lat. Situation; location; e.g., location or place of crime or business. Site: position; the place where a thing is considered, for example, with reference to jurisdiction over it, or the right or power to tax it. It imports fixedness of location. Situs of property, for tax purposes, is determined by whether the taxing state has sufficient contact with the personal property sought to be taxed to jus-*

tify in fairness the particular tax. Town of Cady v. Alexander Const. Co., 12 Wis.2d 236, 107 N.W.2d 672, 676."

27 *"Generally, personal property has its taxable "situs" in that state where owner of it is domiciled. Smith v. Lummus, 149 Fla. 660, 6 Sc.2d 625, 627, 628. Situs of a trust means place of performance of active duties of trustee. Campbell v. Albers, 313 Ill.App. 152, 39 NE.2d 672, 676."* (*Black's Law Dictionary, 6th Edition, page 1387*).

28 "Taxation" is the formal means of paying "tribute" for the protection that government affords.

29 We cannot and should not be compelled to pay for protection that we don't want or don't need; to admit otherwise, is to sanction a government that is a "protection racket"; one that is involved in organized crime and racketeering, one that has an illegal monopoly on protection in violation of the Sherman Antitrust Act.

30 A government that forces you to pay for protection you either don't want or don't need is described in Revelation 19:19 as "the Beast."

31 *"And I saw the beast, the kings* (political rulers) *of the earth, and their armies* (of nonbelievers under a totalitarian democratic form of government), *gathered together to make war against Him* (God) *who sat on the horse and against His army "*

32 By sending such a terrorist government our money, we are fornicating with "the Beast" as described in Revelation. Black's Law Dictionary defines "commerce" as "intercourse".

33 *"Commerce. Intercourse by way of trade and traffic between different peoples of states and the citizens or inhabitant thereof, including not only the purchase, sale, and exchange of commodities, but also the instrumentalities* (governments) *and agencies by which it is promoted and the means and appliances by which it is carried on."* (page 269).

34 - 8 *Beware lest anyone cheat you through philosophy and empty deceit according to the tradition of men* (including through man's deceptive laws written by lawyers), *according*

to the basic principles of the world, and not according to Christ, 9 for in Him dwells all the fullness of the Godhead bodily; 10 and you are complete in Him, who is the head of all principality and power." (*Collosians 2:8-10, bible, NKJV*).

35 We cannot be a friend (domiciliary) of the earth without being an enemy of god.

36 This means that we cannot be a "citizen", "taxpayer" and "resident", all of which maintain an earthly rather than heavenly domicile.

37 *"For our citizenship is in heaven, from which we also eagerly wait for the Savior, the Lord Jesus Christ." (Philippians 3:20, Bible, NKJV*).

38 *"These all died in faith, not having received the promises, but having seen them afar off were assured of them, embraced them and confessed that they were strangers and pilgrims on the earth." (Hebrews 11:13, Bible, NKJV*).

39 *"Beloved, I beg you as sojourners and pilgrims* (temporarily inhabiting in the world), *abstain from fleshly lusts which* war against the soul" (*1 Peter 2:1, Bible, NKJV*).

40 *"Do you not know that friendship* (and citizenship) *with the world is enmity with God? Whoever therefore wants to be a friend* (or "resident") *of the world makes himself an enemy of God." (James 4:4, Bible, NKJV*).

41 *"And do not be conformed to this world, but be transformed by the renewing of your mind, that you may prove what is that good and acceptable and perfect will of God." (Romans 12:2, Bible, NKJV*).

42 If we can't have an earthly "domicile", then we also can't owe "allegiance" to any earthly protector.

43 All protectors of people must be "Servants" and not "Kings" nor "Caesars".

44 May the grace of our Lord Jesus Christ be with you all. Amen.

CHAPTER 15

R ELIGION is "Man's rela-tion to Divinity. To rever-ence, worship, obedience, and submission to mandates and pre-cepts of supernatural or superior beings."

2 "In its broadest sense it in-cludes all forms of belief in the existence of superior beings hav-ing power over human beings by volition, imposing rules of con-duct (law), with future rewards and punishments.

3 "A Bond uniting man to God and a virtue whose purpose is to render God worship due him as source of all being and principle of all government of things. Nikueinikoff v. Archbishop, etc. of Russian Orthodox Greek Catholic Church, 142 Misc. 894, 255 NYS 653, 663." (*Black's Law Dictionary, 6th Edition, page 1292*).

4 The essence of religion is "faith" and "worship".

5 "*Worship. 1. chiefly Brit: a person of importance—used as a title for various officials* (as magistrates and some mayors) *2. reverence offered to a divine be-ing or supernatural power; also: an act of expressing such*

reverence 3. a form of religious practice with its creed and ritual 4. extravagant respect or admiration for or devotion to an object of esteem." (Webster's Ninth New Collegiate Dictio-nary, 1983).

6 The essence of "worship" is obedience to "superior beings".

7 *"He who has* (understands and learns) *My commandments* (laws in the Bible) *and keeps them, it is he who loves Me. And he who loves Me will be loved by My Father, and I will love him and manifest Myself to him." (John 14:21, Bible, NKJV*).

8 *"And we have known and believed the love that God has for us. God is love, and he who abides in love* (obedience to God's Laws) *abides in* (and is a fiduciary of) *God, and God in him." (1 John 4:16, Bible, NKJV*)

9 - 3 *Now by this we know Him* (God*), if we keep His com-mandments. 4 He who says, 'I know Him', and does not keep His commandments, is a liar, and the truth is not in him. 5 But whoever keeps His word, truly the love of God is per-*

fected in him. By this we know that we (His fiduciaries) *are in Him. 6 He who says he abides in Him* (as a fiduciary) *ought himself also to walk just as He* (Jesus) *walked."* (*1 John 2:3-6, Bible, NKJV*).

10 A "fiduciary" is one who owes to another the duties of good faith, trust, confidence, and candor; one who must exercise a high standard of care in maintaining another's money or property.

11 May the grace of our Lord Jesus Christ be with you all, Amen.

CHAPTER 16

THE Bible defines "faith" in these words:

2 *"Now faith is the substance of things hoped for, the evidence of things not seen."* (*Hebrews 11:1, Bible, NKJV*).

3 The product of "faith" is trust and obedience in a "superior being".

4 Faith cannot be supported by physical evidence and therefore cannot be proved in a court of law.

5 The legal field has created its own version of religious "faith" towards the false god of government in the following ways:

6 . . . by using the public schools to teach children to "trust" government as their friend, and to be ignorant (ignore-ant) of God and man's law, and therefore to trust the judges and lawyers about what they may say and must do.

7 . . . by judges preventing law from being discussed in the courtroom in the context of income taxes.

8 Judges sanction litigants who insist on discussing the law.

9 . . . by using "Presumption" as a substitute for evidence.

10 "Presumption" violates the Constitution and "due process rights" of the accused.

11 "Presumption" leads people serving on juries to make decisions based on "what feels good" or based on "public policy" or what the judge commands, instead of what enacted positive law, or the Constitution actually says.

12 "Presumption" causes jurists to commit sin and violate God's Law.

13 The Bible says in Numbers 15:30 that "Presumption" is a grievous sin.

14 Anyone above us, who has more rights or "privileges" than us, is a "superior being", whether it be a judge, public servant, Congressman, etc.

15 This principle is the basis of "equal protection of the law" which is the foundation of our system of jurisprudence.

16 What most people "believe" to be "law" actually is not, but instead is a voluntary private contract (private law) by which they are being deceived by their covetous public servants.

17 The Military Draft is not

"law" for those who do not voluntarily consent.

18 Social Security (Title 42 of the United States Code) is not "law" except for those who voluntarily consent.

19 The Internal Revenue Code, Subtitle A, is not "law" except for those who voluntarily consent.

20 You may be surprised to find out that government has indeed become a secular "Religion".

21 In the worship of God, the "lawgiver" is God.

22 In the worship of Government, the "lawgiver" is the Legislature, or democratic majority.

23 In the worship of God, the "law" is the Bible.

24 In the worship of Government, the "law" is the Constitution; statutes and regulations (in a republic); whatever the judge or ruler says (in an oligarchy, or tyranny).

25 In the worship of God, the "method of worship " is faith, prayer, fasting, service of fellow man/ family; reverencing (respecting) God.

26 In the worship of Government, the "method of worship " is paying income taxes; surrendering rights to judicial jurisdiction and government authority; not questioning or challenging authority; dying in defense of . . . (if serving in the military).

27 In the worship of God, we submit to the "mandates and precepts of God."

28 In the worship of Government, we submit to the "mandates and precepts of Man" (The Beast/Satan).

29 In the worship of God, the "Superior Being" is God.

30 In the worship of Government, the "superior beings" are the President/Legislature/Congress/Mammon (The Beast/Satan).

31 In the worship of God, the "Supreme Being" makes his agents superior in the earth.

32 In the worship of Government, the "superior beings" are not subject to the same laws as everyone else (hypocrisy).

33 In the worship of God, the source of power is "Love = confidence".

34 In the worship of Government, the source of power is "Fear = insecurity".

35 In the worship of God, the rules of conduct are "God's Law

= the Bible or natural Law".

36 In the worship of Government, the rules of conduct are "man's law = statutes".

37 In the worship of God, the future *reward* is "Eternal Life".

38 In the worship of Government, the future *reward* is "absence of IRS harassment for not paying taxes".

39 In the worship of God, the future *punishment* is "slavery to sin = eternal separation from God".

40 In the worship of Government, the future *punishment* is "oppression = harassment for those who challenge government authority".

41 In the worship of God, "love" binds man to the Supreme Being.

42 In the worship of Government, "government-granted privileges; covetousness; limited liability in the case of corporations" bond man to "superior beings".

43 In the worship of God, the object of belief and faith is "trust in God (see Psalm 118:8-9)".

44 In the worship of Government, the object of belief and faith is "trust in self and rulers in their aggrandizement".

45 In the worship of God, influence is spread through "evangelizing".

46 In the worship of Government, influence is spread through "fear, uncertainty, insecurity introduced through media and demagoguery; propaganda; military and political warfare; bribing sheep into submission with government benefits derived from stolen/extorted tax money".

47 In the worship of God, obedience is "If you love me, keep my commandments" (John 14:15).

48 In the worship of Government, obedience is "follow the law or we will throw you in jail and steal your property, fear, and threats.

49 In the worship of God, submission is "knowing that man is not justified by the works of the law but by faith in Jesus Christ, even we have believed in Christ Jesus, that we might be justified by faith in Christ and not by the works of the law; for by the words of the law no flesh shall be justified" (Galatians 2:16).

50 In the worship of Government, submission is "I am a

criminal because no one can obey all of man's laws; there are too many of them".

51 In the worship of God, the principal place of worship is "the Church".

52 In the worship of Government, the principal place of worship is "the Court".

53 In the worship of God, Truth is "sovereign and absolute".

54 In the worship of Government, truth is "relative to whoever is in charge; and whatever corrupted politicians will let corrupted judges get away with before they get removed from office for misconduct".

55 In the worship of God, the method of supporting the "Supreme Being" is the 10% tithe".

56 In the worship of Government, the method of supporting the "superior beings" are taxes/tribute of 50-100%.

57 In the worship of God, power is expanded by "evangelizing".

58 In the worship of Government, power is expanded by obfuscating law; attorney licensing; legal "terrorism" (excessive or unwarranted or expensive litigation); unconstitutional or unlawful but "legal" acts; lies, propaganda, and deceit; judges allowing juries to rule only on facts of each case, and not on the law".

59 Etc.

60 May the grace of our Lord Jesus Christ be with you all. Amen.

CHAPTER 17

I N the Government Church the false "god" is the totalitarian democratic Majority.

2 The judge is the priest.

3 The priest chants the Latin (e.g. *"Ex post facto, malum prohibitum, habeas corpus"*, etc.).

4 The court is the "church" where "worship services" are held.

5 People join the state-sponsored "church" by voluntarily selecting a "domicile" within the territory of the "state" which is the false god.

6 Joining the state-sponsored "church" nominates a "protector" called the "state" which acts as a *man-made substitute* for God's protection.

7 Joining the state-sponsored "church" accepts a man-made law system that replaces and supersedes God's law, and is written by politicians, liars, thieves and Pharisees whom the Bible calls "The Beast" in Revelation 19:19.

8 Licensed attorneys who are "officers of the court" are the "deacons" of the church who conduct the "worship services".

9 The judge's Bench is the "Altar of Baal" (see Judges chapter 6).

10 The judge's Bench is the place where "human sacrifices" are conducted in the name of the false pagan god — the "state".

11 The pleadings are "prayers" to the false god who is the "state", or the state's pretended but not actual representative, the judge.

12 Pleadings" in the United States Supreme Court are called "prayers" even to this day.

13 The Code is the state-sponsored Bible.

14 The Code is an official "statement of public policy" that only becomes "law" for those who volunteer to be subject to it by voluntarily engaging in privileged excise-taxable activities.

15 The "tithes" are "income taxes", also called "tribute", which are unlawfully enforced by a judge whose pay is derived from his theft and plunder of the people.

16 The jury is the twelve disciples of the Judge rather than the Truth or the Law.

17 This is what happens when judges do not permit law to be discussed in the courtroom.

18 The "bailiff" is the deputy of "Baal", who assists in the ritual of human sacrifice that happens daily in courts across the country over income tax issues.

19 Everything that comes out of the mouth of the "priest", which is the judge, becomes "law".

20 *"Judge-made law. A phrase used to indicate judicial decisions which construe away the meaning of statutes, or find meanings in them the legislature never intended. It is perhaps more commonly used as meaning, simply, the law established by judicial precedent and decisions. Laws having their source in judicial decisions as opposed to laws having their source in statutes or administrative regulation." (Blacks' Law Dictionary, 6th Edition, page 841).*

21 The source of law is the god of any society, and therefore the "judge" plays the role of a false pagan god.

22 If law has its source in man's reason, instead of the Bible, then "reason" is the god of that society.

23 If the source of law is an oligarchy, or in a court, senate, or ruler, then that source is the god of that system.

24 Modern humanism, the religion of the state, locates law in the state, and thus makes the state, or the people as they find expression in the state, the god of the system.

25 As Mao Tse Tung has said, *"Our God is none other than the masses of the people".*

26 In Western culture, law has steadily moved away from God, to the people or the state, as its source, although the historic power and vitality of the West has been in biblical faith and law.

27 In any society, any change of law is an explicit or implicit change of religion.

28 Nothing more clearly reveals, in fact, the religious change in a society than a legal revolution.

29 When the legal foundations of a society shift from biblical law to humanism, it means that the society now draws its vitality and power from humanism, not from Christian Theism.

30 No dis-establishment of religion, as such, is possible in any society; a *Church* can be dis-established, and a particular religion can be supplanted by an-

other, but the change is simply to another religion.

31 Since the foundation of law is inescapably religious, no society exists without a religious foundation or without a law-system which codifies the morality of its religion.

32 *"Congress shall make no law respecting the establishment of religion or prohibiting the free exercise thereof."* (First Amendment to the Constitution, and First Article in the Bill of Rights).

33 *The "establishment of religion" clause of the First Amendment means at least this: neither a state nor the Federal Government can set up a church. Neither can pass laws which aid one* (state-sponsored political) *religion, aid all religions, or prefer one religion over another. Neither can force or influence a person to go to or to remain away from church against his will, or force him to profess a belief or disbelief in any religion. No person can be punished for entertaining or professing religious beliefs or disbeliefs, for church attendance or non-attendance. No tax in any amount, large or small, can be levied to support any religious activities or institutions, whatever they may be called, or whatever form they may adopt to teach or practice religion. Neither a state nor the Federal Government can, openly or secretly, participate in the affairs of any religious organizations or groups and vice versa."* (*The US Supreme Court in Everson v. Bd. of Ed., 330 US 1, 15 (1947)*).

34 *"The Establishment Clause is infringed when the government makes adherence to religion relevant to a person's standing in the political community. Direct government action endorsing religion or a particular religious practice is invalid under this approach, because it sends a message to non adherents that they are outsiders, not full members of the political community, and an accompanying message to adherents that they are insiders, favored members of the political community."* (*The US Supreme Court in Wallace v. Jaffree, 472 US 69 (1985)*).

35 The Government agrees that it is a Church.

36 We the People "ordained" the "civil religion" of government; "ordain" is a religious word.

37 *"We the People of the United States, in Order to form a more perfect Union, establish Justice, insure domestic Tranquility, provide for the common defense, promote the general Welfare, and secure the Blessings of Liberty to ourselves and our Posterity, DO ORDAIN AND ESTABLISH this Constitution for the United States of America."* (*Constitution, Preamble*).

38 Washington, D.C, is the "civic temple".

39 *"Now, Mr. Speaker, this Capitol is the civic temple of the people, and we are here by direction of the people to reduce the tariff tax and enact a law in the interest of all the people. This was the expressed will of the people at the polls, and you promised to carry out that will, but you have not kept faith with the American people. (44 Cong.Rec. 4420, July 12, 1909; Congressman Heflin talking about the enactment of the 16th Amendment*).

40 The Judge is "god" — the English jurisprudence that our common law is based upon calls judges, "your worship".

41 (We repeat): *"Worship. 1. chiefly Brit: a person of importance—used as a title for various officials* (as magistrates and some mayors) *2. reverence offered to a divine being or supernatural power; also: an act of expressing such reverence 3. a form of religious practice with its creed and ritual 4. extravagant respect or admiration for or devotion to an object of esteem."* (*Webster's Ninth New Collegiate Dictionary, 1983*).

42 May the grace of our Lord Jesus Christ be with you all. Amen.

CHAPTER 18

A "Cult" is a group of people who worship something other than the true and living God.

2 Any group can become a Cult, including government.

3 "Dangerous Cult" defined:

4 Some cults, or alternative religions, are clearly dangerous: They provoke violence or antisocial acts or place their members in physical, or financial, danger.

5 A few cults have caused the deaths of members through suicide, including mass violence or murder, against people outside the cult.

6 Sociologists note that violent cults are only a small minority of alternative religions, although they draw the most media attention.

7 Dangerous cults tend to share certain characteristics.

8 These groups typically have an exceedingly authoritarian leader (The Federal Judiciary and the IRS) who seeks to control every aspect of members' lives and allows no questioning of decisions.

9 Such leaders may hold themselves above the law or exempt themselves from requirements made of other members of the group or society at large.

10 Such leaders often preach a doomsday scenario that presumes persecution from forces outside the cult (God, in this case, among others) and a consequent need to prepare for an immanent Armageddon, or final battle between good and evil.

11 In preparation they may hoard firearms, or weapons of mass destruction.

12 Alternatively, cult leaders may prepare members for suicide, which the group believes will enhance its place of a better position in the world.

13 The chief characteristics of a "cult" are the following:

14 Cult Leaders think they are a pagan god or have more rights or powers than other members of the group or society.

15 Cult Leaders keep the truth about the inner working of the cult secret from members of the group and outsiders.

16 Cult Leaders preach a doomsday philosophy to keep the people in the group and society stirred up.

17 Cult Leaders encourage

obedience and allegiance to the cult using fear, ignorance, and "presumption" rather than love.

18 Authoritarian rule keeps cult members in subservience to the cult by causing members to donate all or most of their property and time to the cult.

19 May the grace of our Lord Jesus Christ be with you all. Amen.

CHAPTER 19

THE government cult keeps the truth secret from its members

2 This is done by using public schools to dumb down cult members on the subject of law and accountable government, and the voluntary nature of many government codes that are not in fact law.

3 A "cult" is dangerous if it promotes activities that are harmful.

4 Giving away one's earnings and sovereignty is harmful if not done knowingly, voluntarily, and with full awareness of what one is giving up.

5 This is exactly what people do who file or pay monies to the government that no law requires them to pay.

6 Dangerous cults are authoritarian and have mainly "political penalties" for failure to comply.

7 The federal judiciary dishes out stiff penalties to people who refuse to join or participate in the dangerous cult, even though there is no "Law" or positive law authorizing them to do so and no implementing regulation that authorizes any kind of enforcement action for the positive law.

8 These penalties are as follows:

9 Jail time.

10 Persecution from a misinformed jury who has been deliberately tampered with by the judge to cover up government wrongdoing and prejudice the case against the accused.

11 Exorbitant legal fees paying for an attorney in order to resist the persecution.

12 Loss of reputation, credit rating, and influence in society.

13 Deprivation of property and rights to property because of refusal to comply.

14 The dangerous cult of the Internal Revenue Serve Code seeks to control every aspect of the members' lives.

15 The tax code is used as an extensive, excessive, and oppressive means of political control over the spending and working habits of working Americans everywhere.

16 The extent of this political control was never envisioned or intended by our Founding Fathers, who wanted us to be completely free of the government.

17 Members of the cult falsely believe that there is a law requiring them to report every source of earnings, every expenditure in excruciating detail.

18 Members have to sign the report under penalty of perjury and be thrown in jail for three years if even one digit on the report is found by the IRS to be wrong.

19 The IRS, on the other hand, isn't responsible for the accuracy of anything, including their publications, phone support, or even their illegal assessments.

20 In that sense, they are a false god, because they play by different and lesser rules than everyone else.

21 The cult of the Internal Revenue Code also "preaches a doomsday scenario that presumes persecution from forces outside the cult".

22 The Internal Revenue Service is a religion based on fear, and the fear originates from both ignorance about the law, and about what will happen to the members who leave the cult or refuse to comply with all its requirements.

23 The doomsday messages are broadcast from the IRS and DOJ website, public affairs section, where they target famous personalities for persecution because of failure to participate.

24 This indoctrination is no different than what the Communists did in Eastern Europe, where they put a big wall 100 miles long around East Berlin to force people to remain under communist rule.

25 They patrolled the wall by guards, dogs, and weapons, and highly publicized all escape attempts in which people were killed, maimed, or murdered.

26 This negative publicity acted as a warning and deterrent against those who might think of escaping.

27 The cult of the Internal Revenue Code also prepares people for spiritual suicide, and Armageddon.

28 The term "Armageddon" comes from the Bible book of Revelation, where doomsday predictions describe what will happen to those who allow government to become their false god.

29 Those who do so, and who accept the government's "mark"

called the Socialist Security Number will be the first to be judged, persecuted, and injured by the state, according to Revelation.

30 This is the real Armageddon.

31 *"So the first* (angel) *went and poured out his bowl* (of judgment) *upon the earth, and a foul and loathsome sore came upon the men who had the mark of the beast* (the mark of the political rulers) *and those who worshiped his image* (on the money). *" (Revelation 16:2, Bible, NKJV).*

32 Only those who accept the government's mark — UNDER MENTAL PROTEST because of "necessity" — will reign with Christ in Heaven.

33 *"And I saw thrones, and they sat on them, and judgment was committed to them. Then I saw the souls of those who had been beheaded for their witness to Jesus and for the word of God, who had not worshipped the beast* (political rulers) *or his image* (on the money)*, and had not received his mark* (Social Security Number) *on their foreheads of on their hands. And they lived and reigned with*

Christ for a thousand year." (Revelation 20:4, Bible, NKJV).

34 The People created the original federal government in 1789.

35 The government was delegated authority only over EXTERNAL affairs; it did not have any jurisdiction over the INTERNAL affairs of the states of the Union.

37 The government preserved, and enforced the requirement for consent in all human interactions; this is the essence of freedom, justice, and equity.

38 Since 1789, it has gone BAD.

34 It is exceeding its corporate charter, the Constitution, by exercising legislative jurisdiction within the states of the Union, thereby practicing TREASON.

40 It is willfully disobeying "Caesar", which is the People.

41 It is deceiving and enslaving the People using "Words of Art" in the law to confound and confuse.

42 It is refusing to publish court cases in which aspects of its usurpations are challenged by concerned citizens.

43 It is willfully covering up

its wrongdoings.

44 It has turned the tax system into a welfare system for malicious and malingering public dis-servants.

45 It is using public money to fund immoral activities.

46 It is abusing its taxing power for wealth redistribution, like a Robinhood.

47 It is abusing its taxing power to punish success, and reward failure and government dependency with socialist benefits.

48 It is using the federal judiciary to circumvent the sovereignty of the states and to consolidate all power in Washinton, D.C.

49 It is abusing its taxing power to silence churches from challenging its inexorable growth; this has totally broken down the separation of church and state.

50 By virtue of its mis-enforcement of the tax laws, it has become a cancer that is growing out of control and which is therefore a threat to our liberties.

51 It is rapidly transforming itself into an atheistic, totalitarian democratic welfare state.

52 It is making our country into a "welfare magnet" for illegal aliens.

53 It is lying to citizens in its publications about what the tax laws require and the limited extent of its taxing jurisdiction.

54 It has shown by its mis-enforcement of the tax codes and deceitful practices that it loves stealing your money more than it cares about the purpose of its creation, which was to protect and secure your God given rights to life, liberty, and property.

55 May the grace of our Lord Jesus Christ be with you all. Amen.

CHAPTER 20

MOST of the major stuggles in the Bible were against corrupted governments, and excessive taxation.

2 Every time Israel was judged in the Book of Judges, they came under tribute to a tyrannical king.

3 Abraham's great struggles were against overreaching governments. (Genesis chapter 26).

4 Egyptian Pharaohs enslaved God's people. (Exodus chapter 1).

5 Joshua's battle was against 31 kings in Canaan.

6 Israel struggled against the occupation of foreign governments, in the Book of Judges.

7 David struggled against foreign occupation. (2 Samuel chapters 8 and 10).

8 Zechariah lost his life, in 2 Chronicles, for speaking against a king.

9 Isaiah was executed by Manasseh.

10 Daniel was oppressed by officials who accused him of breaking a Persian statutory law.

11 Jesus was executed (crucified) on Calvary hill by a foreign power.

12 Jesus was a victim of Israel's kangaroo court, the Sanhedrin.

13 The last 1/4 of the Book of Acts is about Paul's defense against fraudulent accusations.

14 The last six years of Paul's life was spent in and out prison defending himself against false accusations.

15 May the grace of our Lord Jesus Christ be with you all. Amen.

CHAPTER 21

F OR *where (government) envy and self-seeking (for money government is not entitled to) exist, confusion and every evil thing will be there. (James 3:16, Bible, NKJV).*

2-9 The coming of the lawless one (who is in control of our corrupted government) is according to the working of Satan, with all power, signs, and lying wonders, 10 and with all unrighteous (government and legal profession) deception among those who perish, because they did not receive the love of the truth, that they might be saved. 11 And for this reason God will send them strong delusion, that they should believe the (government) lie, 12 that they all may be condemned who did not believe the truth but had pleasure in unrighteousness." (2 Thess. 2:9-12, Bible, NKJV).

3 May the grace of our Lord Jesus Christ be with you all. Amen.

CHAPTER 22

WHEN your Pastor reads the following Scripture will he miss the word "NOT"?

2 *"When they (Jesus and Peter) were come to Capernaum, they that received tribute money (the tax collectors) came to Peter, and said, Doth* not *your master (Jesus) pay tribute?*

3 *"He (Peter) saith, YES."* (*Matthew 17:24-27*).

4 However, Jesus did *not* pay the temple tax. Jesus was not a taxpayer.

5 *"When he (Peter) was come into the house, Jesus prevented him, saying ... of whom do the kings of the earth take custom or tribute? of their own children, or of strangers? Peter saith unto him, Of strangers. Jesus saith unto him, Then are the children free."* (*Matthew 17:25, 26*).

6 The word "not" is found in all translations of the Bible *except* the New Living Translation, which is obviously intended to mislead.

7 Your Pastor may quote Romans 13:1 and say that you must render taxes to the "governing authorities."

8 However, the Supreme Court said that *we* are the "governing authorites." Caesar is us! Caesar is not our "public servants."

9 Under *this* scenario, *who* should be doing the rendering?

10 "Public servants" should be rendering service to their sovereign-citizen masters.

11 We the people are our own governors, through our representatives, not through our servants in government.

12 Jesus said that the "public servant" cannot be greater than the sovereign-citizen masters.

13 *"No man can serve two masters : for either he will hate the one, and love the other; or else he will hold to the one, and despise the other. Ye cannot serve God and mammon."* (*Matthew 6:24*).

14 May the grace of our Lord Jesus Christ be with you all. Amen.

CHAPTER 23

MOST injustice and corruption within the legal field is done using "clever" definitions to deceive the people, called "words of Art."

2 Read the definitions of words before you read the rest of the law and this will keep you from being deceived.

3 The definitions in the Internal Revenue Code are found at the END of the code, not at the beginning, because government quite frankly doesn't want anyone paying attention to the definitions.

4 Trust your own judgment when you read the law and don't rely on any expert.

5 The Supreme Court says that laws are supposed to be understandable by the common man.

6 After government obfuscates the law using tricky definitions, they will try to convince you that you can't trust your own judgment when reading the law.

7 The use of tricky definitions forces you to rely on corrupt judges and lawyers.

8 Using "Words of Art" puts your liberty in the hands of someone else instead of yourself.

9 The United States Supreme Court said in *Marbury v. Madison* that America is "a society of law, not men."

10 Corrupt government servants are trying to reverse this definition to make us a society of men, not law.

11 The use of "Words of Art" converts judges and lawyers into "witch doctors" and "priests" and government into a "religion", because you have to trust them instead of your own understanding.

12 May the grace of our Lord Jesus Christ be with you all. Amen.

CHAPTER 24

JESUS agreed that the only people who are *"taxpayers,"* are *"strangers"* and not *"sons."*

2 *"Peter answered him, 'From strangers* ("resident aliens" only; *see 26 CFR § 1.1-1(a)(2) (ii) and 26 CFR § 301, 6109-1(d)(3)).*

3 *"Jesus said to him, 'Then the sons* ("citizens" of the Republic, meaning "nationals" and "non-resident aliens") *are free (sovereign* over their own person and labor, e.g., *with SOVEREIGN IMMUNITY)."* *(see Matthew 17:-24-27).*

4 In the Internal Revenue Code, "aliens" (at home in the district United States) are called "residents" — to confuse the common man. (26 USC § 7701(b)(1)(A) Resident alien).

5 According to the IRC, a "resident alien" shall be treated as a resident of the United States with respect to any calendar year if (and only if) such individual meets the requirements of clause (i), (ii), or (iii) :

6 (i) if lawfully admitted for permanent residence. Such individual is a lawful permanent resident of the United States at any time during such calendar year.

7 (ii) if meeting the substantial presence test of paragraph (3)

8 (iii) if electing for such. If such individual elects to be so regarded provided in paragraph (4).

9 In other words: *A person cannot be a "citizen" and a "resident" at the same time because they cannot be an "alien" and a "citizen" at the same time.*

10 Our tax system and the tax system of virtually every country in the world is based on the Maxim, "citizens abroad"/ "aliens at home".

11 "Citizens of the federal United States, abroad", and "aliens at home, in the federal United States" are the ones who are taxed.

12 "Citizens" (under federal law) are people born on federal territory, excluding people born in a state of the Union.

13 May the grace of our Lord Jesus Christ be with you all. Amen.

CHAPTER 25

WHEN a church applies for an Employee Identification Number (EIN) or incorporates as a 501(c)3 "non profit corporation," the church becomes the fleshly authority and de facto Headship of Christ.

3 Before 1940, no church was incorporated with the secular government.

4 Regulating churches began in 1954 with Lyndon Johnson, when Congress enacted Section 501 of the Internal Revenue Code to govern and silence the voice of the Church.

5 In 1954, the Supreme Court ruled in *Brown v. Board of Education, 347 US 483,* that public school segregation of Blacks and Whites was unconstitutional.

6 Lyndon Johnson was later rewarded with the Presidency of the United States in 1963.

7 To be recognized as a religion in the United States, all religious organizations must register with the IRS/FED/STATE TEAM and get a 501(c)3 State "status of exemption" Mark.

8 This goes against what the "government" preaches about "separation of Church and State".

9 Government spokesmen, in this regard, are hypocrites because to be a church you must be controlled by the State that boasts that "Church and State" must not mix.

10 Who, then, is the master, if the State will not recognize the church if it is not licensed by the State?

11 One religion (the State) controls all religions through licensure and through the Crown that controlled all religions before the Revolutionary War.

12 But what if we are under some other type of "government".

13 The Lord said that he set his Church upon "this Rock", meaning that He set *His* Government upon the "Rock", *Christ,* not upon religion or some earthly church.

14 You can see now why the State is telling you that they can't mix the Church (*the Lord's government*) with the State (*the State's religion*).

15 How senseless to think that we are a free people who can worship Almighty God and follow His laws without the Crown interfering and without paying

taxes to a rogue IRS that was not created by the legislature and which operates through fear, extortion, threats, killings, jailings, seizures, suicides, and the like — to keep everyone in bondage to pay tribute to the international elite.

16 So what are Christians in the scheme of things; slaves?

17 Yes, slaves, because most of us fail to realize that the one true Government is the Lord's.

18 Christians have exchanged the God who gave them life, liberty, and peace, for the gods of Mercury and Mars (Commerce and War), so they could engage in commerce and the "privilege" of legalized theft — usury— profit, and debt.

19 Christians have become "hooked" on commerce and the easy life, and have redefined their church to justify it as a *501(c)3 non profit business corporation* registered with and partnered with the state.

20 By their own definition Christians claim to follow the Lord.

21 Okay Christians? then why do you bow down to governors and kings and worship their Constitution as if they and their Constitution could save us, when the Lord commands us Christians to *"not bow down thyself to them, nor serve them"? (Exodus 20:4, Bible, KJV).*

22 *"Thou shalt make no covenant with them, nor with their gods. They shall not dwell in thy land, lest they make thee sin against me: for if thou serve their gods, it will surely be a snare unto thee." (Exodus 23:32-33, Bible, KJV).*

23 This Scripture conflicts with State laws! Why?

24 Christians have abandoned the Lord's Church for the false religion called the State.

25 *"After the doings of the land of Egypt, wherein ye dwelt, shall ye not do: and after the doings of the land of Canaan, whither I bring you, shall ye not do: neither shall ye walk in their ordinances. Ye shall do my judgments, and keep mine ordinances, to walk therein: I am the Lord your God." (Leviticus 18:3-4, Bible, KJV).*

26 Why must our churches have a 501(c)3 tax exemption from the IRS, the collection agent for private, non-federal Federal Re-

serve Bank?

27 Why are pastors compromising the most important church principle in Scripture, the Headship and authority of Christ (Eph 1:19) by making the government the de facto head of the church corporation.

28 Are we "citizens of the State"? or are we "servants of the Lord"?

29 Churches register as 501(c)3 business corporations on the advise of esquire attorneys. They are not real churches, according to law, they are non-profit *business corporations* that owe their existence to the State.

30 This is one reason why the church is small in the affairs of the world. She is basing her existence on a worldly "John" rather than "Jesus Christ".

31 May the grace of the Lord Jesus Christ be with you all. Amen.

CHAPTER 26

ACCORDING to the IRS, it-self, 501(c)3 non-profit corporations cannot legally...

1 ...expose conspiracies;

2 ...criticize the New World Order;

3 ...criticize any politician; Republican or Democrat;

4 ...criticize government agencies and bureaus; such as the IRS, FBI, BATF, CIA, EPA, DEA, OSHA, DOJ, NAFT, GATT, FEMA, NSA;

5 ...criticize any institution of government; such as the White House, the Congress, the Federal Reserve Board, or the Supreme Court;

6 ...encourage citizens to call or write to their congressmen, senators, governor, mayor, or other public officials;

7 ...criticize any proposed or pending bill or legislation that would take away the rights and freedoms of the people;

8 ...make disparaging remarks about or criticize any other non-profit corporations, faith, cult, or religion;

9 ...expose or criticize the New Age Movement;

10 ...support or encourage a law-abiding militia;

11 ...support or encourage the Second Amendment — the right of the people to keep and bear arms;

12 ...discourage young women from getting an abortion or endorse the pro-life movement;

13 ...teach that abortion, especially partial birth abortion, is murder and is the killing of innocent babies;

14 ...identify homosexuality as a sin and an abomination to God;

15 ...express an opinion on any politically incorrect subject or issue;

16 ...appeal to people's emotions by employing an evangelization method (such as "fire and brimstone" preaching) not considered a "reasoned approach" by the IRS;

17 ...discuss or identify threats to Christianity;

18 ...discuss subjects or topics the IRS deems "sensationalist";

19 ...criticize well-known public figures or institutions that the IRS deems "worthy", such as the super-rich elite, international bankers, the Hollywood movie industry;

20 ...publish or broadcast in-

formation on any topic without giving credence to the opposing viewpoints of Christ's enemies;

21 ...publish books, tapes, or products that expose the elitist plot against humanity and God;

22 ...criticize the Pope or the Vatican, or contrast the New Catholic Catechism with the truths found in the Holy Bible (note that only liberal churches are permitted by the IRS to criticize the Catholic Church);

23 ...criticize the United Nations or other such globalist groups as the Council on Foreign Relations, the Builderbergers, and the Trilateral Commission;

24 ...criticize the Masonic Lodge, the Order of Skull & Bones, or other Secret Societies;

25 ...highlight or otherwise bring attention to the immorality of public officials or corruption in government;

26 ...complain of government wrongdoing or injustice, such as happened at Waco, Ruby Ridge, Oklahoma City, and elsewhere;

27 ...criticize the Jewish ADL or other Jewish lobby groups;

28 ...support home schooling, home churches, or unregistered churches;

29 ...spend money on missionary projects or charitable causes not approved by the IRS;

30 ...promote or encourage alternative healthcare (herbs, vitamins, prayer, etc.);

31 ...expose false teachings of any kind by anyone;

32...support or encourage persecuted Christians suffering under anti-Christian regimes in Red China, Cuba, Russia, Israel, Saudi-Arabia, the United states, and elsewhere;

33 ...ordain a pastor whose training or qualifications are not approved by the IRS;

34 ...advocate or teach any Bible doctrine that is politically or religiously incorrect, or is inconsistent with any "public policy," such as abortion, feminism, gay rights, etc., currently being enforced by the IRS.

35 Americans have freedom of religion, freedom of speech, and freedom of the press — just so long as their religion, speech, and publications remain "politically correct".

36 May the grace of our Lord Jesus Christ be with you all. Amen.

CHAPTER 27

THE leading cause of false church doctrine is ignorance and a disregard of the law.

2 What does God say about pastors who won't read or learn and follow either God's or man's law?

3 *"One who turns his ear from hearing the law* (God's law or the Supreme law of the Land, the Constitution)*, even his prayer is an abomination."* (*Proverb 28:9, Bible, NKJV*).

4 Not only are the prayers of Pastors who refuse to read and learn or obey God's Law and man's law an abomination, but they make the prayers of those in their congregation/flock into an abomination as well.

5 They make every act to follow church leadership into an abomination.

6 When our leadership is deceived, then everyone suffers.

7 The judgment of the Lord begins in His House.

8 *"For the time has come for judgment to begin at the house of God; and if it begins with us first, what will be the end of those who do not obey the gospel of God?"* (*1 Peter 4:17,*

Bible, NKJV).

9 Those stewards who maintain His house must ensure that teachers are held to a stricter standard than members of the Household.

10 *"My brethren, let not many of you become teachers, knowing that we shall receive a stricter judgment."* (*James 3:1, Bible, NKJV*).

11 May the grace of our Lord Jesus Christ be with you all. Amen.

CHAPTER 28

THE purpose of law is to "define and limit" the power of both the government and private individuals.

2 This is the essence of how the law protects us and why we should obey the law.

3 *"The history of liberty is the history of the limitation of governmental power, not the increase of it." (Woodrow Wilson, President of the United States).*

4 *"Sovereignty itself is, of course, not subject to law, for it is the author and source of law; but in our system, while sovereign powers are delegated to the agencies of government, sovereignty itself remains with the people, by whom and for whom all government exists and acts. And the law is the definition and limitation of power. It is, indeed, quite true that there must always be lodged somewhere, and in some person or body, the authority of final decision; and in many cases of mere administration, the responsibility is purely political, no appeal lying except to the ultimate tribunal or the public judgment, exercised either in the pressure of opinion,*

or my means of the suffrage." (*Yick Wo v. Hopkins, 118 US 356 (1886)).*

5 Any believer who refuses to learn AND obey the law, is voting in favor of NO LIMITS on the power of our "public servants".

6 *"Those who are too smart to engage in politics* (or law) *are punished by being governed by those who are not smart enough." (Plato).*

7 Individuals, including judges, lawyers, and public servants CANNOT be trusted with power or to hold *themselves* accountable to the law.

8 *"Who polices the police?"*

9 *"Absolute power corrupts absolutely".*

10 Americans are asleep at the wheel in overseeing and supervising their public servants because they refuse to learn and follow both God's law and man's law and to vigorously stand up for liberty.

11 May the grace of our Lord Jesus Christ be will you all. Amen.

CHAPTER 29

ACCORDING to U.S. Congress, the essence of being a "communist" is a disregard for the constitutional limits on the authority of our government.

2 TITLE 50 > CHAPTER 23 > SUBCHAPTER IV > Sec. 841: *- Findings and declarations of fact".*

3 *"The Congress finds and declares that the Communist Party of the United States* (consisting of the IRS, DOJ and a corrupted federal judiciary)*, although purportedly a political party, is in fact an instrumentality of a conspiracy to overthrow the (de jure) Government of the United States* (and replace it with a the *de facto* government that now exists and is ruled by the judiciary).

4 *"It constitutes an authoritarian dictatorship* (IRS, DOJ in collusion with a corrupt judiciary) *within a* (constitutional) *republic, demanding for itself the rights and privileges* (including immunity from prosecution for their wrongdoing in violation of Article 1, Section 9, Clause 8 of the Constitution) *accorded to political parties, but denying to all others the liber-*ties guaranteed by the Constitution.

5 *"Unlike political parties, which evolve their policies and programs through* (consensual) *public means, by the reconciliation of a wide variety of individual views, and submit those policies and programs to the electorate at large for approval or disapproval, the policies and programs of the Communist Party are secretly prescribed for it* (by corrupt judges and the IRS in complete disregard of the tax laws) *by the foreign leaders of the world Communist movement* (the IRS and Federal Reserve).

6 *"Its members* (the Congress which was terrorized to do the biddings of the IRS by recently framing Congressman Traficiant) *have no part in determining its goals and are not permitted to voice dissent to party objectives.*

7 *"Unlike members of political parties, members of the Communist Party are recruited for indoctrination* (in the public schools by liberals, socialists, and homosexuals) *with respect to its objectives and methods, and are organized, in-*

17

structed, and disciplined (by the IRS and a corrupted judiciary) *to carry into action slavishly the assignments given them by their hierarchical chieftains.*

8 *"Unlike political parties, the Communist Party* (thanks to a corrupted federal judiciary) *acknowledges* (whether deliberately or through apathy and ignorance) *no constitutional or statutory limitations upon its conduct or upon that of its* members.

9 *"The Communist Party is relatively small numerically, and gives scant indication of capacity ever to attain its ends by lawful political means.*

10 *"The peril inherent in its operation arises not from its numbers, but from its failure to acknowledge any limitation as to the nature of its activities, and its dedication to the proposition that the present constitutional Government of the United States ultimately must be brought to ruin by any available means, including resort to force and violence* (and using the income tax).

11 *"Holding that doctrine, its role as the agency of a hostile*

foreign power (the Federal Reserve and American Bar Association) *renders its existence a clear present and continuing danger to the security of the United States.*

12 *"It is the means whereby individuals are seduced into the service of the world Communist movement, trained to do its bidding, and directed and controlled in the conspiratorial performance of their revolutionary services. Therefore, the Communist Party should be outlawed. (50 USC 23, Section 841).*

13 Americans who don't know or don't individually enforce the limits placed on the government by the Constitution or the law enacted pursuant to it, are COMMUNISTS at heart.

14 Has YOUR legal ignorance and apathy, or a deficient government public education made YOU into a communist and a SHEEP of the system?

15 You ARE if you don't know the law and don't hold your public servants accountable.

16 May the grace of our Lord Jesus Christ be with you all. Amen.

CHAPTER 30

THE "hypocrisy and law-lessness" that Jesus so ve-hemently criticized flourishes in our government today.

2 *"Woe to you scribes and Pharisees* (politicians and law-yers in modern day times), *hypo-crites! For you are like white-washed tombs which indeed ap-pear beautiful outwardly, but inside are full of dead men's bones and all uncleanness. Even so you also outwardly ap-pear righteous to men, but in-side you are full of hypocrisy and lawlessness."* (*Matthew 23:27-28, Bible, NKJV*).

3 The reason our government continues to flourish is because of our own political and legal apathy and ignorance.

4 *"The only thing necessary for evil to triumph is for good men to do nothing or to trust bad men to do the right thing."*

5 All of the damage done by Sa-tan described in the Parable of the Wheat and the Tares hap-pened while the farmer was "asleep".

6 *"The kingdom of heaven is like a man who sowed good seed in his field; but while men slept,* *his enemy came and sowed tares among the wheat and went his way."* (*Matthew 13:24-25, Bible, NKJV*).

7 A prosperous economy has not only made Americans into obese couch potatoes who are *physically* asleep, but a failing government-run educational sys-tem has put them to sleep *intel-lectually* as well in respect to the very serious violations of the Constitution and enacted law that our government is blatantly in-volved in.

8 Prosperity is a disease that inflects us all with apathy.

9 May the grace of our Lord Jesus Christ be with you all. Amen.

CHAPTER 31

G OD'S judgment begins in God's House.

2 *"For the time has come for judgment to begin at the house of God; and if it begins with us first, what will be the end of those who do not obey the gospel of God?"* (*1 Peter 4:17, Bible, NKJV*).

3 - 1 *Where do wars and fights come from among you? Do they not come from your desires for pleasure* (unearned money from the government) *that war in your members* (and in your democratic governments)? *2 You lust* (after other people's money) *and do not have. You murder* (the unborn to increase your standard of living) *and covet* (the unearned) *and cannot obtain* (except by empowering your government to steal for you). *You fight and war* (against the rich and the nontaxpayers to subsidize your idleness). *Yet you do not have because you do not ask* (the Lord, but instead ask the deceitful government). *3 You ask and do not receive, because you ask amiss, that you may spend it on your* (hedonistic) *pleasures. 4 Adulterers and adulteresses! Do you not know that friendship* (or "citizenship" or "Domicile") *with the world* (or the governments of the world) *is enmity with God? Whoever therefore wants to be a friend of the world* (or of the governments or atheists of the world) *makes himself an enemy of God."* (*James 4:1-4, Bible, NKJV*).

4 Whether we sin because of omission or commission is immaterial; either way, if we violate God's law or surrender our sovereignty to a false god or idol, including government, then we are jeopardizing our salvation.

5 - 11 *Because you* (Solomon, the wisest man who ever lived) *have done this, and have not kept My covenant and My statutes* (violated God's laws), *which I have commended you, I will surely tear the kingdom* (and all your sovereignty) *away from you and give it to your* (public) *servant."* (*1 Kings 11:9-13. Bible, NKJV*).

6 *"Humble yourselves in the sight of the Lord, and He will lift you up (above govern-*

ment)." (James 4:10, Bible, NKJV).

7 *"Those people who are not governed by God* (and His law, both figuratively and literally) *will be ruled by tyrants." (William Penn after which Pennsylvania was named).*

8 Christians who abdicate their role as God's servants or who let governments equal or exceed God in influence over their lives have created a false god and are practicing idolatry.

9 Our present tax crisis of taking more than 50% of our income is God's judgment on America.

10- *21 The Lord is well pleased for His righteousness' sake; He will exalt the law* (His law, not man's law) *and make it honorable. 22 But this is a people robbed and plundered* (by the IRS)*! All of them are snared in* (legal) *holes* (by the sophistry of greedy lawyers)*, and they are hidden in prison houses; they are for* (government) *prey, and no one delivers; for* (IRS) *plunder, and no one says, "Restore!" 23 Who among you will give ear to this? Who will listen and hear for the time to come? 24 Who gave Jacob for plunder, and Is-*

rael to the robbers? (IRS). *Was it not the Lord, He against whom we have sinned? For they would not walk in His ways, nor were they obedient to His law, 25 Therefore He has poured on him the fury of His anger and the strength of battle; it has set him on fire all around, yet he did not know; and it burned him, yet he did not take it to heart." (Isaiah 42:21-25, Bible, NKJV).*

11 *"Has the Lord as great delight in burnt offerings and sacrifices, as in obeying the voice of the Lord* (and the people in the Constitution)*? Behold, to obey is better than sacrifice, And to heed than the fat of rams. For rebellion* (of either the Constitution or the Bible) *is as the sin of witchcraft, And stubbornness is as iniquity and idolatry. Because you have rejected the word* (and laws) *of the* (sovereign) *Lord* (or "We the People" in the Constitution)*, He also has rejected you from being king* (and sovereign over your government as a private citizen, or a public servant)*." (1 Samuel 15:22-23, Bible, NKJV).*

12 Nehemiah confessed the sins of the nation; he recognized that

Israel was enslaved:

"Here we are, [slaves] today! And the land that You gave to our fathers, To eat its fruit and its bounty, Here we are, [slaves] in it! And it yields much increase to the kings You have set over us, Because of our sins; Also they have dominion over our bodies and our cattle At their pleasure: And we are in great distress." (*Nehemiah 9:36-37, Bible, NKJV*).

13 The Babylonian IRS ruled over their person and their property, and the *"abundant produce"* of the land was going to a foreign power. He also states the reason for that slavery, *"Because of our many sins"*.

14 Jesus affirmed this reason when he said, *"Most assuredly, I say to you, whoever commits sin is a slave of sin."* (*Jesus, at John 8:34, Bible, NKJV*).

15 The Evangelist, Billy Graham said in 1958 that if God doesn't destroy America He will have to apologize for Sodom and Gomorrah; we believe Billy Graham was wrong.

16 In His judgment on nations, God does not annihilate them as much as He subjects them to "tribute".

17 God's discipline of the nation was recognized because the nation's wealth was going to a foreign empire.

18 Could it be that the income tax on the American family today is the direct result of our nation's sins?

19 ... that America has become "disobedient and rebelled against" YHWH while bowing down to statism and government idolatry?

20 Congress' findings on Communism forcefully proves that this is precisely the case.

21 He who has an ear, let him read again and ponder this report.

22 Why aren't preachers preaching this?

23 Why do they not recognize that the income tax is a judgment on America putting everyone under "tribute" for making an idol out of government and the IRS?

24 Well, there are very few preachers who look at the Bible politically; most of the preachers look at the Word only spiritually.

25 Most preachers have reduced the Scripture down to a set of personal, spiritual conflicts.

They fail to see that the present political structures and systems of taxation in this country are tools the enemy uses to keep Christianity poor and powerless, and weakening daily as a relevant political force in society.

26 As the Church goes, so goes the Nation.

27 In the competition between "church" and "state" for the affections of the people, Christians are simply and rapidly being displaced and eclipsed by an overarching "social insurance company" called "government" that has replaced the church as a monopolistic provider of "social services".

28 The individual, once the only sovereign in our formerly republican system of government, has been replaced by the "state". Humanism is the "Neo-god".

29 Ironically, Christians and churches are subsidizing and embracing this erosion of their political power by participating in a deceptive tax system that is actually voluntary and unenforceable, but which our covetous public servants, lusting after power and money, have deceived Christians into believing is "mandatory", when it is not.

30 May the grace of our Lord Jesus Christ be with you all. Amen.

CHAPTER 32

DID Jesus come to "turn the other cheek?"

2 - 34 *"Do not think that I came to bring peace on earth. I did not come to bring peace but a sword.* 35 *"For I have come to 'set a man against his father, a daughter against her mother, and a daughter against her mother-in-law'; 36 "and 'a man's enemies will be those of his own household.' 37 "He who loves father or mother more than Me is not worthy of Me. 38 "And he who does not take his cross and follow after Me is not worthy of Me. 39 "He who finds his life will lose it, and he who loses his life for My sake will find it."* (*Matthew 10:34-39, Bible, NKJV*).

3 America will be the land of the free when it becomes the home of the brave.

4 What are you doing to educate the flock about government deception and usurpation?

5 If we aren't risking our peace as believers, then we aren't growing and will lose our liberties eventually to a false god called government.

6 *"Power concedes nothing without a demand. It never did, and it never will. Find out just what the people will submit to and you have found out the exact amount of injustice and wrong which will be imposed upon them; and these will continue till they have resisted with either words or blows, or by both. The limits of tyrants are prescribed by the endurance of those whom they suppress."* — Fredrick Douglas, 1849.

7 *"Turn the other cheek"?*

8 Back in the days of Jesus, the Roman "Masters" were the undisputed rulers of man on earth — undisputed by all except Jesus and his followers of course.

9 The accepted practice was, if you encountered a Roman soldier on your way and there was some mild altercation between you and he, that he would strike you upon the cheek, often wearing a glove (*like a latter day challenge to a duel*).

10 The "proper" response was for you, the "peasant", to immediately kneel, bow your head, exposing the back of your head. This or course signaled submission. If the anger was not

quenched by this display of subservience, you were to prostrate yourself, putting your forehead against the ground, and the Roman soldier would place his heel on the back of your head. (Ever hear of the saying: "Under the heel of Rome"?)

11 But along came Jesus who said, essentially, don't kneel to Rome, don't bow before earthly authority; bow only to the Father in Heaven.

12 *"Whosoever shall smite thee on thy right cheek, turn to him the other also";* an act of resistance to the tyranny of Rome.

13 All the outreaches and charity in the world will not accomplish justice because the government is taking over social welfare with money it is stealing from Christians.

14 Churches cannot and will not win the war to bribe the poor with stolen money.

15 Government is competing with God for the affections of the people.

16 Churches cannot win this war by mixing church and state and encouraging growth in government.

17 The best worship services in the world will not solve this problem.

18 *"Behold, to obey is better than sacrifice, And to heed than the fat of rams. For rebellion is as the sin of witchcraft, And stubbornness is as iniquity, and idolatry. Because you have rejected the word* (and laws) *of the Lord, He also has rejected you from being king* (and sovereign over your government)." (*1 Samuel 15:22-23. Bible, NKJV*).

19 The essence of worship is JUSTICE THROUGH OBEDIENCE throughout the week, not praise only on Sundays.

20 Only courage and conviction and morality and Christian confrontation will solve this problem.

21 *"He has shown you, O man, what is good; And what does the Lord require of you But to do justly. To love mercy, And to walk humbly with your God?"* (*Micah 6:8, Bible, NKJV*).

22 *"The violence of the wicked will destroy them because they refuse to do justice."* (*Proverb 21:7, Bible. NKJV*).

23 We cannot be Holy in God's eyes unless we leave our com-

fort zone and do what other people are not willing to do to fix this situation.

24 *"And you shall be holy to Me, for I the Lord am holy, and have separated you from the peoples, that you should be Mine." (Leviticus 20:26, Bible, NKJV).*

25 The Supreme Court explained our American Heritage.

26 Our religious heritage is not one of conformity, but rebellion:

27 *"This case involves a cancer in our body politic* (democracy, greed and wickedness and covetousness of our elected and appointed servants on a massive scale, see James 1:19-27 and Psalm 94:16-23). *It is a measure of the disease which afflicts us. Army surveillance, like Army regimentation, is at war with the principles of the First Amendment. Those who already walk submissively will say there is no cause for alarm. But submissiveness is not our heritage. The First Amendment was designed to allow rebellion to remain as our heritage. The Constitution was designed to keep government off the backs of the people. The Bill of Rights was added to keep the precepts of belief and expression, of the press, of political and social activities free from surveillance. The Bill of Rights was designed to keep agents of government and official eavesdroppers away from assemblies of people. The aim was to allow men to be free and independent and to assert their rights against government. There can be no influence more paralyzing of that objective than Army surveillance. When an intelligence* (or IRS) *officer* (with a computer and the aid of a SSN) *looks over every nonconformist's shoulder in the library, or walks invisibly by his side in a picket line, or infiltrates his club* (or forces him to submit an income tax return and then scrutinizes it for personal information or illegal activity), *the America once extolled as the voice of liberty heard around the world is no longer cast in the image which Jefferson and Madison designed, but more in the Russian* (Communist) *image, depicted in Appendix III to this opinion. (Laird v. Tatum, 408 IS 1; 92 S.Ct. 2318 (1972))*.

28 *"We have no government*

armed with the power capable of contending with human passions unbridled by morality and religion. Avarice (greed), ambition, revenge, or gallantry (debauchery), would break the strongest cords of our Constitution as a whale goes through a net.

29 *"Our Constitution was made only for a moral and religious people. It is wholly inadequate to the government of any other."* — John Adams, 2nd President of the United States.

30 You can't be a "friend" (*a " ("taxpayer"; "citizen"; or "resident")* of the world as a Christian.

31 *"Adulterers and adulteresses! Do you now know that friendship* (and "citizenship") *with the world* (or the governments of the world) *is enmity with God? Whoever therefore wants to be a friend* ("citizen" or "taxpayer" or "resident") *of the world makes himself an enemy of God."* (*James 4:4, Bible, NKJV*).

32 We cannot serve God and Government (mammon).

33 *"No servant* (or religious ministry or biological person)

can serve two masters; for either he will hate the one and love the other, or else he will be loyal to the one and despise the other. You cannot serve God and mammon (government). *" (Jesus in Luke 16:13, Bible, NKJV).*

34 *"For all the nations* (including especially people in fallen and deceived churches) *have drunk of the wine of the wrath of her* (Babylon, the Great Harlot) *fornication, the kings of the earth* (the Beast, see Rev. 19:19) *have committed fornication* ("intercourse/"commerce") *with her* (by participating in a corrupted tax system), *and the merchants of the earth have become rich through the abundance of her luxury."* (*Revelation 18:3, Bible, NKJV*).

35 Instead we are "aliens" or "nonresident aliens" of the corporate United States.

36 *"These all died in faith, not having received the promises, but having seen them afar off were assured of them, embraced them and confessed that they were strangers and pilgrims on the earth."* (*Hebrews 11;13, Bible NKJV*).

37 *"Beloved, I beg you as*

sojouners and pilgrims (temporarily occupying the world), *abstain from fleshly lusts which war against the soul."* (*1 Peter 2:1, Bible, NKJV*).

38 Christians are "nationals" but not "citizens" under federal law.

39 *"For our citizenship is in heaven* (and not earth), *from which we also eagerly wait for the Savior, the Lord Jesus Christ."* (*Philippians 3:20, Bible, NKJV*),

40 Christians are "foreign ambassadors" from the foreign state called "Heaven".

41 A Christian's house is a "foreign embassy" and a Christian has "diplomatic immunity" from federal jurisdiction.

42 A Christian can not have an earthly "domicile" because all of a Christian's protection comes only from God and His sovereign laws.

43 We cannot stand idly by and continue to subsidize with our "donations" (which the government has deceived Christians into thinking are "taxes"), participate in or associate with, the destruction of our freedoms and religious icons in our society.

44 Our government has become a "protection racket" that has forced every man, woman, and child into economic servitude, with the illegal enforcement of income tax laws, the loss or privacy and violation of rights (driver's licensing), and invasion of privacy with information sharing between branches of the government and private business.

35 The cost of "protection" is "subjection".

46 God and His laws are the only source of permanent protection for Christians.

46 Christians have a moral and biblical responsibility to correct this deception.

47 Christians cannot claim to love their neighbor as themselves if they tolerate such abuse of their neighbor by their government.

48 Christians cannot allow the government to "establish" itself as a church and a cult, and replace faith" with "presumption" and misplaced trust.

49 *"And I heard another voice from heaven saying, 'Come out of her* (Babylon the Great Harlot, and atheistic totalitarian democracy where government is a false god), *my people, lest you*

share in her sins, and lest you receive of her plagues.'"

50 Let's get to work!

APPENDIX

EPISTLE to the AMERICANS I

CHAPTER 33

I N the United States Code, the **United States** [U.S.] is defined to mean ONLY the **District of Columbia** (see 26 USC 7701(a)(9)).

2 And in all IRS publications, the term **U.S.** [United States] means ONLY the **District of Columbia**.

3 In this context the **United States** is the **seat of the Government of the United States** [of America] referred to in the Constitution, over which Congress has been given the power **"to exercise exclusive legislation in all cases whatsoever"** and **"to make all laws which shall be necessary and proper for carrying into execution the forgoing powers"** itemized in Article I, Section 8, of the American Constitution.

4 We can ALSO say that this **area**, meaning the **District of Columbia United States** or the **United States District of Columbia**, is part of the **federal United States** otherwise known as the **federal zone.**

5 Why is it important to have a proper understanding of the definition of these terms? Because the **states of the Union** are **foreign** to the federal jurisdiction of the **United States** — unless we *voluntarily* concede that they are not.

6 The Internal Revenue Code (IRC) describes only two separate types of excise tax; **a municipal tax** and **an income tax.**

7 The **municipal tax** is assessed upon the *citizens and residents* of the **United States** — meaning the municipal **United States District of Columbia** under Subtitles A, B, and C of the IRS code.

8 The **income tax** is assessed upon *domestic and foreign corporations* of the **United States** under Subtitle D.

9 Anyone who is neither a **U.S. citizen** (a person born in the District of Columbia or in a U.S. territory) nor a **resident** living in the District of Columbia, is a **nonresident alien** under the IRC — is a **nonresident alien of the corporate United States.**

10 **Nonresident aliens** are **nonresidents** of the legislative jurisdiction of most federal laws and in most cases are **nontaxpayers under the IRC** — whether they know this or not —

unless they *voluntarily* concede that they are not.

11 **Taxpayers** only have to pay income taxes on wages received from *within* **the District of Columbia**; on the profits of domestic or foreign corporations registered *within* **the District of Columbia**, and on earnings from property and investments *within* **the District of Columbia**.

12 **Nationals** are **Nonresident aliens** of the United States under 8 USC 1101(a)(21), but NOT **aliens** of the United States of America.

13 Americans domiciled in the non-federal areas of the 50 Union states are **nonresident aliens** of the **federal United States** and its Internal Revenue Code — whether they know it or not — and therefore have no **U.S.** source of income unless they work for the federal U.S. government as public officers or have passive investments *within* the District of Columbia United States.

14 The **United States** includes no other places than the **District of Columbia**.

15 *"A citizen of a possession of the United States (except Puerto Rico and Guam) . . . is treated . . . as if he were a **nonresident alien** individual."* (see 26 CFR 1.931-1, "Status of citizens of U.S. possessions").

16 *"An individual is a **nonresident alien** if such individual is neither a citizen of the United States nor a resident of the United States (within the meaning of subparagraph (A)."* (see 26 USC 7701(b)(1)(B), "Nonresident alien").

17 Americans born in states of the Union (i.e., in the United States of America), and domiciled there, are not **citizens of the United States** under the Internal Revenue Code or any federal law of the United States; they are **Citizens of the United States of America**.

18 They are not **residents** either, because **residents of the United States are aliens of the United States of America, according to the Internal Revenue Code.** Consequently, the only other status that most Americans have under the Internal Revenue Code is the status of **nonresident aliens of the United States**.

19 Within the Internal Revenue

Code the term "**nonresident alien**" is a **word of art**. This term has a special use different from what common sense and common logic dictates — just as the term "**employee**" in the Internal Revenue Code is a **word of art** which means **an elected or appointed official of the U.S. government** (see 26 USC 3401(c) and 26 CFR 31.340(c)). The terms **alien** and **nonresident alien** are also defined in the regulations, at 26 CFR 1.441-1(c).

20 The above two definitions are the only definitions of **individual alien, and nonresident alien** found in 26 CFR.

21 A natural person who lives *inside* the 50 states of the Union (*outside* of the federal zone) can be a **nonresident alien** without being an **alien** — which at first glance would appear to be a contradiction.

22 How can a person be a **nonresident alien** without being an **alien**?

23 Because a **nonresident alien** as defined in 26 USC 7701(b)(1)(B) is someone who is not a **U.S. citizen or resident** — which is what a **national but not citizen is**, as defined in 8 USC 1101(a)(21) and 1101(a)(22) (B).

24 That same **national** can't be an **alien** because **aliens** cannot be **citizens and nationals** at the same time according to 26 CFR 1.1441-1(c)(3)(i).

25 The terms **U.S. National** and **noncitizen U.S. National** are equivalent and interchangeable.

26 An examination of IRS Form 1040NR confirms the fact that **U.S. Nationals are indeed nonresident aliens**.

27 Our federal government has tried to confuse sovereign citizens so that they would **discount** being sovereign citizens. The term **nonresident alien** is a contradiction deliberately designed by lawyers to confuse us and obfuscate (make obscure) the truth.

28 All **residents of the United States** can only be **aliens under the Internal Revenue Code.** When we call someone a **nonresident** we are saying he is NOT an **alien** — "non" means "not". Therefore, when we call someone a **nonresident alien** we are calling him a **non-alien alien**. How's this for **cognitive dissonance** (things you don't really understand)?!! Whew!

29 Since lawyers know that people will avoid **cognitive dissonance**, they intentionally named the term the way they did to confuse you.

30 If Congress were honest about the definitions they use, they would have used the term **nonresident national** or **foreign national** instead of **nonresident alien** in 26 CFR 1.1441-1(c)(3)(i) — and told you that this status under the Internal Revenue Code applies to people born in one of the states of the Union.

31 They would have *then* given away the **hoax** and shown the average American that **he is not liable for the income tax** unless he receives gross income from sources *within* **the federal United States** that fall under 26 CFR 1.861-8(f), which most people do not.

32 Pivotal to the **nonresident alien** position is the definition of the word **income** and our identity as **natural persons which are not corporations**.

33 The term **nonresident alien** in the context of the federal income tax encompasses those individuals who are state but not federal citizens — who are **foreigners of the United States living in the United States of America**.

34 One can be a **natural born sovereign state citizen and a national of their county** and not be a **U.S. citizen under the acts of Congress or the IRS**. Such ones are **nationals or state nationals or American nationals**.

35 The Treasury Department has admitted in its publications that **state nationals are indeed nonresident aliens**.

36 The famous Supreme Court Case *Brushaber v. Union Pacific Railroad,* 240 US 1 (1916) involved a French immigrant who was a **citizen of New York state** but not a **U.S. citizen under Federal law**. Therefore, he was a **national but not a citizen** under 8 USC 1101(a)(22)(B) and 8 USC 1452.

37 He brought suit against the Union Pacific Railroad to enjoin them from paying income taxes to the federal government on the excuse that it was reducing the corporate earnings of shareholders located in the states of the Union and therefore constituted a **direct tax**.

38 The Supreme Court said that it would not interfere with the decision of the corporation to *voluntarily* **pay income taxes** even though the law did not require the corporation to do so.

39 Shortly after that finding of the Supreme Court, the Treasury Department published Treasury Decision 2313 in which they identified Mr. Brushaber as a **nonresident alien** of the United States.

40 "Well, why does it matter whether I'm a **U.S. citizen** or a **nonresident alien** anyway," you might ask? "Either way, you say I'm not liable for the income tax because **there is no liability statute or implementing regulation permitting enforcement of Subtitle A income taxes imposed in 26 USC 1.**"

41 That's a very good question. There is NO advantage to being a **U.S. citizen**, but a big DISadvantage because once you *volunteer* to become a **statutory "U.S. citizen"** under 8 USC 1401 you *volunteer* to be **completely subject to the jurisdiction of the U.S. government and the federal courts**.

42 Our federal government is covetous of obtaining as much of our assets as it can get, using deceit and fraud.

43 *"Both before and after the 14th Amendment of the federal Constitution, it has not been necessary for a person to be a citizen of the United States in order to be a citizen of his state."* (*U.S. v. Cruikshank*, supra).

44 **A national, state national, natural born sovereign, and/or nonresident alien** are the best status we sovereigns under God can claim to be, because this will give our liberties the most protection against the encroachments of greedy Congressmen, unscrupulous IRS agents, and corrupt federal judges.

45 *"A prudent man foresees evil and hides himself, but the simple pass on and are punished. By humility and fear of the Lord are riches and honor and life. Thorns and snares are in the way of the perverse; he who guards his soul will be far from them."* (Prov. 22:3).

46 May the grace of our Lord Jesus Christ be with you all. Amen.

CHAPTER 34

W E explained in the previous Chapter that people born in the states of the Union are **nationals** or **state nationals** under 8 USC 1101(a)(21).

2 To confuse us for tax purposes, **nationals** are classified as **nonresident aliens** as defined in 26 USC 7701(b)(1)(B).

3 The term **United States** as used above means the **District of Columbia**.

4 A **nonresident alien** is **nonresident** to the **United States** as defined in the Internal Revenue Code at 26 USC 7701(a)(9) and (a)(10), which simply means that he does not live in the **District of Columbia: the federal United States: the federal zone,** for short.

5 There is no way to interpret the definition of the "**United States**" other than meaning the **District of Columbia** for the purposes of Subtitle A, federal income taxes.

6 The Constitution and federal law both confine all persons holding public office to residing in the **District of Columbia**. (U.S. Constitution, Article 1, Section 8, Clause 17).

7 *"**All offices attached to the seat of government shall be exercised in the District of Columbia, and not elsewhere,** except as otherwise provided by law."* (Title 4, Chapter, 3, Section 72).

8 A **nonresident alien** who does not hold a public office in the United States government **is not responsible for income tax withholding** under Subtitle C of the Internal Revenue Code **or for federal income taxes** under Subtitle A of the Internal Revenue Code. People not holding public office also **cannot be levied upon** under 26 USC 6331(a).

9 All income **not effectively connected with a trade or business in the United States** or earned from labor outside the **federal zone of the federal United States** is **exempt** from inclusion as gross income and **exempt** from withholding. (see 26 CFR 31.3401(a)(6)-1 Remuneration for services of nonresident alien individuals).

10 A portion of the regulation above is confirmed by the statutory rules for computing taxable income found in 26 USC 861.

11 *"Compensation for labor or*

services performed in the United States shall not be deemed to be income from sources within the United States if the compensation is for labor or services performed as an employee of or under a contract with a nonresident alien, foreign partnership, or foreign corporation, not engaged in trade or business within the United States."

12 The word **trade or business** above is defined in the Internal Revenue Code as **the functions of a public office — an elected or appointed office in the United States** or a federal instrumentality. The *only* proper subjects of the income tax are government contractors, agencies, and public officers.

13 *"The term trade or business includes the performance of the functions of a public office."* (26 USC 7701 (a)(26), "Definitions").

*14 "The essential characteristics of a **public office** are:*

(1) Authority conferred by law.

(2) Fixed tenure of office.

(3) Power to exercise some of the sovereign functions of government.

*(4) Key element of such test in that the **officer is carrying out a sovereign function.***

*(5) Essential elements to establish public position as **public office** are:*

(a) Position must be created by Constitution, legislature, or through authority conferred by legislature.

(b) Portion of sovereign power of government must be delegated to position.

(c) Duties and powers must be defined directly or implied, by legislature or through legislative authority.

(d) Duties must be performed independently without control of superior power other than law.

(e) Position must have some permanency."

(Black's Law Dictionary, Sixth Edition, p.1230.

15 What's more, a person can only earn **wages** if he is an **"employee"**: an **elected or appointed officer of the United States government** under 26 CFR 31.3401(c)-1.

16 The only other way he can earn **wages** is to have a **volun-**

tary withholding agreement in place called a W-4. If he never **volunteered,** then he didn't earn **wages**.

17 If a private employer *coerces* his employee to sign a W-4 under duress, that doesn't count as *volunteering* because in that instance he had a choice of either starving to death or committing perjury under penalty of perjury on a W-4 form.

18 *"In the general course of human nature, A POWER OVER A MAN'S SUBSISTENCE AMOUNTS TO A POWER OVER HIS WILL."* (Alexander Hamilton, Federalist Paper, No. 79).

19 The tendency of employers to *coerce* their employees into essentially becoming liars just so they can feed themselves and their families explains the following comment:

20 *"The income tax has made more liars out of the American people than golf."* — Will Rogers.

21 The only taxable source of income of **nonresident aliens** would be income **effectively connected with a trade or business within the "United States"**.

22 Sources **other than income effectively connected with a trade or business in the United States** are *excluded* by law from taxation, because they are not explicitly *included* in any implementing regulation.

23 This is a requirement of statutory construction within the legal field, which says — *"express-io unius est exclusio alterius* — the expression of one thing is the exclusion of another. Mention of one thing implies exclusion of another."* (Black's Law Dictionary, sixth edition, page 581).

24 Without a regulation to implement the provisions of 26 USC 871(a) that has been published in the federal register, there is no basis to conclude that income not derived from sources **effectively connected with a trade or business in the United States** is taxable income for persons who are not **federal employees**.

25 In fact, Anything that is not published in the federal Register may not apply to anything but federal employees. (see 44 USC 1505(a)). No statute within the

Internal Revenue Code is enforceable unless it also has implementing regulations.

26 *"Neither the statute not the regulations are complete without the other; **only together do they have any force in effect**, therefore the construction of one necessarily involves the construction of the other." (U.S. v. Mersky,* 361 US 431 (1960)).

27 **Nonresident aliens** who do not hold public office in the United States government do not earn taxable income and therefore need not withhold, and need not file any federal tax return.

28 Some people hear the word **nonresident alien** and assume that it only means **foreigners**. But how can a **foreigner** from another country serve in a public office of the United States government when the Constitution requires that the President must be a **"Natural Born Citizen"** and senators and representatives must be **"Citizens of the United States"** ?

29 **Natural Born Citizens** are **Citizens of the United States of America** and people born in states of the Union.

30 These people are **nonresi-**dent aliens in Subtitle A of the tax code because the tax code only has force and effect *within* **the federal zone** which is limited to the District of Columbia, the territories and possessions of the United States, and the federal areas or enclaves within states of the Union.

31 These are the only natural people that the income tax applies to, based on 26 CFR 1.861-8(f)(1)(iv).

32 The income tax collected under the authority of Subtitle A of the Internal Revenue Code is simply a **federal employee kickback** disguised to "look" like a tax.

33 But in fact, the legislative intent of the 16th Amendment revealed by President Taft's speech before Congress clearly shows the purpose of Subtitle A of the Internal Revenue Code as simply a tax on **federal government employees** and nothing more.

34 This **federal employee kickback** disguised as a legitimate **income tax on everyone** was begun in 1862 during the exigencies of the Civil War and has continued with us ever since. (Congressional Record, Senate,

June 16, 1909, pages 3344-3345).

35 The rather deceptive **Payroll Compliance Manuals** of today aren't actually telling a lie but they leave the most important points about the **non-tax liability of nonresident aliens** undisclosed. People born in states of the Union are **nonresident aliens** under the tax code.

36 This lack of disclosure results in a **constructive fraud** and leaves the average reader, who is a **nonresident alien** who was born in a state of the Union, with the *incorrect presumption* that he has a legal obligation to *voluntarily* participate in a corrupt and usurious **federal employee kickback program**.

37 The authors of these **Payroll Compliance Manuals** would have their licenses to practice law or their CPA certifications pulled by the IRS or by a federal Judge whose retirement benefits depend on maintaining the fraudulent and oppressive tax system we live under today, if they told the whole truth.

38 May the grace of our Lord Jesus Christ be with you all. Amen.

CHAPTER 35

THE government has a vested interest to maximize the number of **taxpayers**. Their authority to impose an income tax has as a prerequisite — **domicile within the United States** as defined in 26 USC 7701(a)(9) and (a)(10) to include only the **District of Columbia** and is not expanded elsewhere under IRS Subtitle A to include **states of the Union**.

2 People born and domiciled within states of the Union are **nationals** or **state nationals** and not **statutory U.S. citizens**.

3 They are **Citizens of the united States of America** under 8 USC 1401 but NOT **citizens of the United States** under the 14th Amendment.

4 The only real taxpayers on an IRS form 1040 are **aliens of the united States of America** of one kind or another.

5 IRS Publication 7130 says that the only people who can use IRS form 1040 are **citizens and residents of the United States**, both of whom have in common a **domicile within the District of Columbia**.

6 Collectively, **citizens and residents of the United States** having a **domicile within the District of Columbia** are called **U.S. persons** and are defined in 26 USC 7701(a)(30).

7 Therefore the government has a vested interest in making **nonresident aliens** in states of the Union into **resident aliens** in the United States.

8 They do this on the basis of the **Collective Entity Rule**.

9 The U.S. Supreme Court has repeatedly held that the mandate of the **5th Amendment**, which protects **persons** from compulsory self-incrimination, applies only to **natural persons**, not **fictional persons** such as limited and general partnerships, limited liability companies, and other **corporations**.

10 Therefore, corporations, partnerships, limited partnerships, limited liability companies, and other kinds of **business organizations** are treated differently from **individuals** for **5th Amendment** purposes.

11 The **Collective Entity Rule** was first articulated in *Hale v. Henke* (201 US 43, 26 S.Ct. 370, 50 L.Ed.652).

12 In that case, a corporate of-

ficer, who had been served with a **subpoena duces tecom** (a court order that **must** be complied with) commanding the production of corporate records and books, claimed a **5th Amendment bestowed privilege** (not a right) against the production of the corporate records and books. The *Hale* Court denied the claim of a privilege, opining that:

13 *"We are of the opinion that there is a clear distinction between an **individual** and a **corporation**, and the latter has no right to refuse to submit its papers and books for examination at the suit of the State."*

14 *Hale* made it clear that **a corporation** has no **5th Amendment privilege** that insulates the <u>Collective Entity</u> from producing its corporate records and books. The Court's rationale was that, **because the corporation** . . .

15 *". . . is a creature of the state, it receives certain special privileges and franchises, and holds them subject to the laws of the state and the limitations of its corporate charter. Its powers are limited by law. It would be a strange anomaly to hold*

that a state, having chartered a corporation to make use of certain franchises, could not, in the exercise of its sovereignty, inquire how these franchises had been employed, and whether they had been abused, and demand the production of the books and papers for that purpose."

16 However, the *Hale* Court did not decide whether a **corporate officer** or **custodian of records** could refuse to produce corporate documents by invoking his or her personal 5th Amendment privilege.

17 Very recently the Supreme Court held in *United States v. Hubbell* (120 S.Ct. 2037 (2000)) that interrogatories and depositions of **natural persons** are protected under the <u>Collective Entity Rule</u>, clearly distinguishing between you and me as **natural persons,** and a **fictional person** who is subject to an internal revenue tax.

18 This principle of the <u>Collective Entity Rule</u> was recently applied in Tax Court by former IRS agent Larry Becraft in his defense in stopping the government from compelling the pro-

duction of documents protected by his **5th Amendment privilege**. There are other cases also in this regard such as *Baltimore City DSS v. Bouknight* (1990) and *Brasswell v. United States* (1988).

19 **Who or what are you?** Are you a **legal piece of paper**, a **birth certificate**, a **legal fiction person**, — or are you a **natural person** and **human being**?

20 **Corporation**: *"An artificial 'person' or legal entity created by or under the authority of the laws of a state. An association of persons created by statute as a legal entity. The law treats the corporation a*s a *'person'* whi*ch can sue and be sued."* — Black*'s Law Dictionary.*

21 Therefore, as a **legal person** under the laws of the state, rather than a **natural person** under the law of God, you are treated as a **legal fiction: a corporate person: a corporation:** as **property** belonging to the State.

22 As a **natural person**, you are presumed to have **voluntarily agreed** (contracted) to become the **"surety"** —co-signer — for a **government created**

corporation over which it has total control . . . of a **legal fiction person** having the same name as your's but printed in the **all caps name** of the **legal corporation** that it is.

23 This **corporate strawman** is created, owned, and controlled by the **corporate United States** and you are presumed to be an **"accommodation party"** to the deal.

24 **Accommodation party**: *"A person who, without compensation or other benefit, signs a negotiable instrument for the purpose of being a surety for another party (called the accommodated party) to the instrument. • The accommodation party can sign in any capacity (i.e., as maker, drawer, acceptor, or indorser). An accommodation party is liable to all parties except the accommodated party, who impliedly agrees to pay the note or draft and to indemnify the accommodation party for all losses incurred in having to pay it."* (Black's Law Dictionary, 7th Edition, p.16).

25 In other words, the government has **authorized** you to be responsible for your **ens legis**

(meaning, government created) **entity strawman**. Therefore, as long as you act the part as though you are responsible for your **ens legis entity strawman** the **adhesion contract** is affirmed by your action.

26 **Adhesion contract**: *"A standard form contract prepared by one party, to be signed by the party in the weaker position, usually a consumer, who has little choice about the terms."* (Black's Law Dictionary, 7th Edition, p.318).

27 Every time you sign a check as the **authorized party for your ens legis entity strawman**, you unknowingly affirm the government's **false legal presumptions** concerning you, — and you affirm the lie.

28 Look closely at the line on your bank-checks beneath where you sign your name. That line (marked MP) is the **micro-print signature line** above which you sign your name as the **accommodation party**, which reads in tiny *micro-print letters,* "authorized signature authorized signature authorized signature authorized signature, etc" affirming that you are the **accommodation party** for your **ens legis entity strawman**.

29 Every time you sign your name on any document you are **affirming and accommodating** this government **hoax**.

30 The first Hebrew word in Genesis is 'B'Bay-sheet': *"In the beginning."*

31 All that existed *"in the beginning"* was the Elohim, the Word; there was nothing before this Elohim, the Christ.

32 When the Elohim began to create, all that was created was created of the Elohim; everything is from this one Source. Nothing exists outside of and without the Elohim, nor can it ever be otherwise.

33 After each period of creation, the Creator, Elohim, pronounced that which He created, as good.

34 On the sixth evolving period of creation ("day") you will read in the King James Version of the Bible, *"So God created man in his own image, in the image of God he created him; male and female he created them. And God blessed them."* (Genesis 1:27).

35 In the Hebrew version it says that the Creator, Elohim, the Christ, created souls on the sixth

day, in his/her image and likeness, or sameness; each soul having aspects of both male and female energy.

36 The souls were pronounced good and blessed by the Creator, Elohim.

37 Not only is the word "soul" missing from the King James Version, so is the word "good" missing, in reference to the souls that were pronounced good.

38 In Genesis 2, the Lord God (Jehovah), not to be confused with the Creator, Elohim, made a body for the soul and placed the soul into the body, and man became a living being, or **natural person**. You are a living soul in human form also known as a **natural person**.

39 A NATURAL PERSON CANNOT BE TAXED FOR THE MERE PRIVILEGE OF EARNING A LIVING.

40 According to the **Constitution** you are one of **"the People"** who created the federal government.

41 It is self-evident that the government is created as a **paper fiction**, and that you are a **natural person**.

42 From the government's point of view, your **strawman** is the government's **corporate, person, property, slave** and you are **his legal agent** who is authorized to act, speak, and co-sign papers for him as his **legal guardian**.

43 Your journey from freedom to slavery began when you applied for *your strawman's* **Social Security Number** and checked the box that said, *"Check here if you are a U.S. citizen."* By checking the box, **you were joined to the paper fiction** created by the State.

44 According to 26 CFR 1-1.1(C) . . .

45 *"Every person born or naturalized in the United States and subject to its jurisdiction is a citizen."* — 26 CFR 1-1.1(C).

46 Do you get it? Remember, there are two main definitions of the words United States (or united States).

47 When the **United States** is written with a capital **U** and **S** it is referring to the **Washington, D.C., district of Columbia United States**, created by and under the authority of **Congress**.

48 The use of the words **"subject to its jurisdiction"** should tell you that a **"citizen"** is under

the authority of, and the corporate ownership of the **United States.**

49 For most **natural persons** the SSN is their **first contact** with the federal government.

50 Pretty stupid on our part not to know this, but very slick on the part of the lawyers and politicians who would bind us into slavery on the State Plantation.

51 But relax, this is the nexus point, the loophole that will save you. But things get worse before they get better; darkness proceeds the dawn.

52 Your **second contact** with the federal government was when you *voluntarily* displayed *your strawman's* **Social Security Number** when 'his' first employer asked you to fill out a W-4 form.

53 In filling out the W-4 form, you entered your number of dependents as "**1**". . . and skipped past item 7 . . .

54 "I claim exemption from withholding for (*the particular year*) and I certify that I meet both of the following conditions for exemption.

55 • Last year I had a right to a refund of all Federal income tax withheld because I had **no tax liability**.

56 • This year I expect a refund of all Federal income tax withheld because I expect to have **no tax liability**.

57 • If you meet both conditions, write '<u>exempt</u>' here"

58 If you have **no tax liability** you don't need withholding.

59 Without exception everywhere you look in the IRS Code and every single Federal Court case dealing with taxation what is being taxed are **corporations, corporate persons, and property of the government engaged in a taxable activity**.

60 The activity your strawman and you as his partner are engaged in, according to 'his' **Individual Master File (IMF)** on file with the IRS, has something to do with a source that is taxable such as alcohol, tobacco, or firearms.

61 Alcohol, tobacco, and firearms are the only sources **within the states** that the Federal government can tax, according to the Constitution. And get this: your strawman is presumed to be engaged in one of these source activities in Puerto Rico, Guam, or the Virgin Islands.

62 To verify that your strawman has income from a taxable source, and that 'he' is engaged in a taxable activity in Puerto Rico, Guam, or the Virgin Islands, use the Freedom of Information Act (FOIA) to get a copy of *your strawman's* **Individual Master File** from the IRS.

63 The office of the U.S. Attorney General has for years falsely claimed that the 16th Amendment to the Constitution gave Congress the power to tax personal income, and that the personal income tax is a direct tax that does not have to be apportioned . . .

64 . . . but based on the case history of the Supreme Court, the only tax referred to in the 16th Amendment is an **excise tax that doesn't have to be apportioned**. What kind of tax is that? **An indirect tax.**

65 The U.S. Supreme Court has said that the purpose of the 16th Amendment has been used to frighten us into believing that Congress was given a special power to tax our wages without having to describe a harmful, taxable activity or identify an activity that needs to be regulated, or set a direct tax to be apportioned among the states.

66 Big government was created out of this mythical tax. To this day no one has found an excise called an income tax that would apply to most individuals.

67 The Internal Revenue Code is full of excise taxes.

68 There are taxes on making airline flights, telephone calls, fishing rods, tires, liquor, fuel, cigars, snuff, outboard motors, bows and arrows, gasoline, gas guzzler cars, etc.

69 **What you won't find however is a tax on the activities that produce your income.**

70 Lawful taxation of regulated industries and harmful activities helps to secure our Rights to Life, Liberty and the Pursuit of happiness, but taxation of our God given rights reduces us to slavery.

71 Before the income tax, we were free to choose whether we would be taxed or not. The law was clear.

72 After 1913, big government began its cancerous growth.

73 The income tax grew by fraud, intimidation and deceit. Making you *believe* that you owe a tax and then *coercing* you into

paying what you do not owe, by threatening to put you in prison if you don't, *is genuine tax fraud.*

74 **The Declaration of Independence** is the first and most important part of our organic law. This great document firmly establishes the source of our individual rights and our sovereignty.

75 **Our only duty and Right, as a free people, is to throw off government that,** *"evinces a Design to reduce [us] under absolute Despotism".*

76 We owe no other duty to government. Our Constitution limits government in order to protect and maintain our freedom.

77 National taxation is limited to four taxes: **direct taxes, imposts, duties**, and **excise taxes**. No national tax is proper that cannot be made to fit the mold of the four taxes.

78 The 16th Amendment is a further limitation of the power of Congress to tax. After the ratification of the amendment, **an income tax cannot be a direct tax.**

79 If an **income tax** is to be imposed among the several states it must be in the form of one of the remaining three indirect taxes. The **excise** is the only choice since it regularly produces income of some kind.

80 The King of Great Britain caused the dissolution of its political connection with the American States by his many injurious acts, including, *"imposing Taxes on us without our Consent."*

81 Congress created an **"income tax"** that does not fit within the mold established by the Constitution. Such a tax may only be imposed upon us **with our consent.**

82 A voluntary yielding to the will of another is necessary for **valid consent.** Such consent is an act of reason attended by due deliberation, exercised only after consideration of the values and benefits offered on each side.

83 The blind execution of tax agreements **under the penalty of perjury** without sufficient tax knowledge and under duress is an *act of neglect* when committed by an uninformed citizen, but an *act of cowardice* when committed by a citizen who is in-

formed.

84 May the grace of our Lord Jesus Christ be with you all. Amen.

CHAPTER 36

IN the United States Code, the **United States** [U.S.] is defined to mean ONLY the **District of Columbia** (see 26 USC 7701(a) (9)).

2 And in all IRS publications, the term **U.S.** [United States] means ONLY the **District of Columbia.**

3 In this context the **United States** is the **seat of the Government of the United States** [of America] referred to in the Constitution, over which Congress has been given the power "**to exercise exclusive legislation in all cases whatsoever**" and "**to make all laws which shall be necessary and proper for carrying into execution the forgoing powers**" itemized in Article I, Section 8, of the American Constitution.

4 We can ALSO say that this **area**, meaning the **District of Columbia United States** or the **United States District of Columbia**, is part of the **federal United States** otherwise known as the **federal zone.**

5 Why is it important to have a proper understanding of the definition of these terms?

6 Because the **states of the Union** are **foreign** to the federal jurisdiction of the **United States** — unless we *voluntarily* concede that they are not.

7 The Internal Revenue Code (IRC) describes only two separate types of excise tax; **a municipal tax** and **an income tax.**

8 The **municipal tax** is assessed upon the *citizens and residents* of the **United States** — meaning the municipal **United States District of Columbia** under Subtitles A, B, and C of the IRS code.

9 The **income tax** is assessed upon *domestic and foreign corporations* of the **United States** under Subtitle D.

10 Anyone who is neither a **U.S. citizen** (a person born in the District of Columbia or in a U.S. territory) nor a **resident** living in the District of Columbia, is a **nonresident alien** under the IRC — is a **nonresident alien of the corporate United States.**

11 **Nonresident aliens** are **nonresidents** of the legislative jurisdiction of most federal laws and in most cases are **nontaxpayers under the IRC** — whether they know this or not —

unless they *voluntarily* concede that they are not.

12 **Taxpayers** only have to pay income taxes on wages received from *within* the District of Columbia; on the profits of domestic or foreign corporations registered *within* the District of Columbia, and on earnings from property and investments *within* the District of Columbia.

13 **Nationals** are **Nonresident aliens** of the United States under 8 USC 1101(a)(21), but NOT **aliens** of the United States of America.

14 Americans domiciled in the non-federal areas of the 50 Union states are **nonresident aliens** of the **federal United States** and its Internal Revenue Code — whether they know it or not — and therefore have no **U.S.** source of income unless they work for the federal U.S. government as public officers or have passive investments *within* the District of Columbia United States.

15 The **United States** includes no other places than the **District of Columbia**.

16 *"A citizen of a possession of the United States (except Puerto Rico and Guam) . . . is treated . . . as if he were a nonresident alien individual."* (see 26 CFR 1.931-1, "Status of citizens of U.S. possessions").

17 *"An individual is a nonresident alien if such individual is neither a citizen of the United States nor a resident of the United States (within the meaning of subparagraph (A)."* (see 26 USC 7701(b)(1)(B), "Nonresident alien").

18 Americans born in states of the Union (i.e., in the United States of America), and domiciled there, are not **citizens of the United States** under the Internal Revenue Code or any federal law of the United States; they are **Citizens of the United States of America**.

19 They are not **residents** either, because **residents of the United States are aliens of the United States of America, according to the Internal Revenue Code.** Consequently, the only other status that most Americans have under the Internal Revenue Code is the status of **nonresident aliens of the United States**.

20 Within the Internal Revenue

Code the term "**nonresident alien**" is a **word of art**. This term has a special use different from what common sense and common logic dictates — just as the term "**employee**" in the Internal Revenue Code is a **word of art** which means **an elected or appointed official of the U.S. government** (see 26 USC 3401(c) and 26 CFR 31.340(c)).

21 The terms **alien** and **nonresident alien** are also defined in the regulations, at 26 CFR 1.441-1(c).

22 The above two definitions are the only definitions of **individual alien, and nonresident alien** found in 26 CFR.

23 A natural person who lives *inside* the 50 states of the Union (*outside* of the federal zone) can be a **nonresident alien** without being an **alien** — which at first glance would appear to be a contradiction.

24 How can a person be a **nonresident alien** without being an **alien**?

25 Because a **nonresident alien** as defined in 26 USC 7701(b)(1)(B) is someone who is not a **U.S. citizen or resident** — which is what a **national but not citizen is**, as defined in 8 USC 1101(a)(21) and 1101(a)(22) (B).

26 That same **national** can't be an **alien** because **aliens** cannot be **citizens and nationals** at the same time according to 26 CFR 1.1441-1(c)(3)(i).

27 The terms **U.S. National** and **noncitizen U.S. National** are equivalent and interchangeable.

An examination of IRS Form 1040NR confirms the fact that **U.S. Nationals are indeed nonresident aliens**.

28 Our federal government has tried to confuse sovereign citizens so that they would **discount** being sovereign citizens.

29 The term **nonresident alien** is a contradiction deliberately designed by lawyers to confuse us and obfuscate (make obscure) the truth.

30 All **residents of the United States** can only be **aliens under the Internal Revenue Code.** When we call someone a **nonresident** we are saying he is NOT an **alien** — "non" means "not". Therefore, when we call someone a **nonresident alien** we are calling him a **non-alien alien**. How's this for **cognitive disso-**

nance (things you don't really understand)?!! Whew!

31 Since lawyers know that people will avoid **cognitive dissonance**, they intentionally named the term the way they did to confuse you.

32 If Congress were honest about the definitions they use, they would have used the term **nonresident national** or **foreign national** instead of **nonresident alien** in 26 CFR 1.1441-1(c)(3)(i) — and told you that this status under the Internal Revenue Code applies to people born in one of the states of the Union.

33 They would have *then* given away the **hoax** and shown the average American that **he is not liable for the income tax** unless he receives gross income from sources *within* **the federal United States** that fall under 26 CFR 1.861-8(f), which most people do not.

34 Pivotal to the **nonresident alien** position is the definition of the word **income** and our identity as **natural persons which are not corporations**.

35 The term **nonresident alien** in the context of the federal income tax encompasses those individuals who are state but not federal citizens — who are **foreigners of the United States living in the United States of America**.

36 One can be a **natural born sovereign state citizen and a national of their county** and not be a **U.S. citizen under the acts of Congress or the IRS**. Such ones are **nationals or state nationals or American nationals**.

37 The Treasury Department has admitted in its publications that **state nationals are indeed nonresident aliens**.

38 The famous Supreme Court Case *Brushaber v. Union Pacific Railroad,* 240 US 1 (1916) involved a French immigrant who was a **citizen of New York state** but not a **U.S. citizen under Federal law**. Therefore, he was a **national but not a citizen** under 8 USC 1101(a)(22)(B) and 8 USC 1452.

39 He brought suit against the Union Pacific Railroad to enjoin them from paying income taxes to the federal government on the excuse that it was reducing the corporate earnings of shareholders located in the states of the

Union and therefore constituted a **direct tax**.

40 The Supreme Court said that it would not interfere with the decision of the corporation to *voluntarily* **pay income taxes** even though the law did not require the corporation to do so.

41 Shortly after that finding of the Supreme Court, the Treasury Department published Treasury Decision 2313 in which they identified Mr. Brushaber as a **nonresident alien** of the United States.

42 "Well, why does it matter whether I'm a **U.S. citizen** or a **nonresident alien** anyway," you might ask? "Either way, you say I'm not liable for the income tax because **there is no liability statute or implementing regulation permitting enforcement of Subtitle A income taxes imposed in 26 USC 1**."

43 That's a very good question. There is NO advantage to being a **U.S. citizen**, but a big DIS-advantage because once you *volunteer* to become a **statutory "U.S. citizen"** under 8 USC 1401 you *volunteer* to be **completely subject to the jurisdiction of the U.S. government and the fed-eral courts**.

44 Our federal government is covetous of obtaining as much of our assets as it can get, using deceit and fraud.

45 *"Both before and after the 14th Amendment of the federal Constitution, it has not been necessary for a person to be a citizen of the United States in order to be a citizen of his state."* (*U.S. v. Cruikshank*, supra).

46 **A national, state national, natural born sovereign, and/or nonresident alien** are the best status we sovereigns under God can claim to be, because this will give our liberties the most protection against the encroachments of greedy Congressmen, unscrupulous IRS agents, and corrupt federal judges.

47 *"A prudent man foresees evil and hides himself, but the simple pass on and are punished. By humility and fear of the Lord are riches and honor and life. Thorns and snares are in the way of the perverse; he who guards his soul will be far from them."* (Prov. 22:3).

48 May the grace of our Lord Jesus Christ be with you all.

CHAPTER 37

DOJ Dismisses Felony Tax Prosecution - *With Prejudice* - After PRA Defense Raised Evidence OMB Complicit In Income Tax Fraud DOJ & IRS Petitioned To Explain.

2 On May 12, 2006 in Peoria, Illinois, the attorney for the U.S. Department of Justice (DOJ) begged the court to dismiss all charges against IRS victim Robert Lawrence in federal District Court.

3 The motion for dismissal came on the heels of a surprise tactic by Lawrence's defense attorney Oscar Stilley.

4 The tactic threatened exposure of **IRS's on-going efforts to defraud the public.**

5 The move put DOJ attorneys in a state of panic that left them with only one alternative: beg for **dismissal, with prejudice.**

6 Stilley's tactic paid off.

7 Sixty days earlier, the DOJ had indicted Lawrence on **three counts of willful failure to file** a 1040 form, and **three felony counts of income tax evasion.**

8 The federal Judge dismissed all charges *with prejudice*, meaning the DOJ cannot charge

Lawrence with those crimes again.

9 The trial was to have started on Monday morning, May 15, 2006.

10 On Wednesday, May 10, Stilley mailed a set of documents to the DOJ in response to DOJ's discovery demands.

11 The documents revealed to DOJ for the first time that Lawrence was basing his entire defense on an act of Congress, 44 U.S.C. 3500 – 3520, also known as the **Paperwork Reduction Act (PRA)**.

12 In Section 3512 of the Act, titled **"Public Protection,"** it says that no person shall be subject to any penalty for failing to comply with an agency's collection of information request (such as a 1040 form), if the request does not display **a valid control number** assigned by the Office of Management and Budget (OMB) *in accordance with the requirements of the Act*, or if the agency fails to inform the person who is to respond to the collection of information that he is not required to respond to the collection of information request unless it displays **a valid control**

number.

13 In Section 3512 Congress went on to authorize that the **protection** provided by Section 3512 may be raised in the form of a complete defense at any time during an agency's *administrative process* (such as an IRS Tax Court or Collection and Due Process Hearing) or during a *judicial proceeding* (such as Lawrence's criminal trial).

14 In sum, the PRA requires that all government agencies display **valid OMB control numbers** and certain disclosures directly on all information collection forms that the public is requested to file. **Lawrence's sole defense was he was not required to file an IRS Form 1040** because it displays an invalid OMB control number.

15 Government officials knew that if the case went to trial, it would expose the **fraudulent, counterfeit 1040.** They also must have known that a trial would expose the **ongoing conspiracy** between OMB and IRS to publish 1040 forms each year that those agencies knew were in violation of the PRA. That would raise the issue that the Form

1040, with its **invalid control number**, is being used by the Government to cover up the underlying **constitutional tort** — the enforcement of a direct, unapportioned tax on the labor of every working man, women and child in America.

16 **Any information collection form,** such as IRS Form 1040, which lacks *bona fide* statutory authority or **which conflicts with the Constitution, cannot be issued an OMB control number.** If a control number were issued for such a form, the form would be invalid and of no force and effect.

17 Under the facts and circumstances of the last 24 years, it is safe to say that **IRS Form 1040 is a fraudulent, counterfeit, bootleg form.**

18 Government officials responsible for this fraud should be investigated and face indictment for willfully making and sponsoring false instruments.

19 Caught between a rock and a hard place, the DOJ and IRS decided **not to let the Lawrence case proceed** because it would reveal one critical and damning fact:

20 The PRA law protects those who fail to file IRS bootleg Form 1040.

21 The DOJ knew that it stood a significant chance of losing the case, and if that happened, **the press and others would quickly spread the word**, and leave only fools to ever file a 1040 again. Oscar Stilley's pleadings and documents made these points quite clear:

22 • IRS Form 1040 violates the federal Paperwork Reduction Act (PRA) and is therefore a legally invalid form.

23 • Under the Public Protection clause of the PRA, no person can be penalized for failing to file a 1040 if the IRS fails to fully comply with the PRA.

24 • The PRA statutes explicitly provide that a PRA challenge is a complete defense and can be raised in any administrative or judicial proceeding.

25 • The IRS Individual Form 1040 has not and cannot comply with the requirements of the PRA because no existing statute authorizes the IRS to impose or collect the federal income tax from individuals. That lack of *bona fide* authority makes it impossible for IRS to avoid violating the PRA.

26 *The Brunswick Disparch* has researched the facts, law and circumstances surrounding this case, and has determined that:

27 • A public trial would have opened a "Pandora's Box" of legal evidence and government testimony under oath that would establish the IRS 1040 form as both fraudulent and counterfeit.

28 • Oscar Stilley's PRA defense "checkmated" the DOJ and IRS

29 • The Office of Management and Budget (OMB) appears to have been complicit with IRS in deceiving the public and in helping perpetuate the 1040 fraud by promulgating federal regulations that negate the plain language of the PRA laws passed by Congress and by allowing the IRS to continually skirt the explicit requirements of those statutes.

30 May the grace of our Lord Jesus Christ be with you all.

CHAPTER 38

YOU may be wondering why the **Joe Banister victory over the IRS** was not reported on television, radio or in newsprint.

2 A classic ***David v. Goliath*** victory of monumental proportions literally took over Internet this past year for several days, yet virtually no mention of it had been reported by the mainstream media.

3 Was this deliberate?

4 If you were even suspicious of the quality of the news we have been receiving for the past 15 years, this ***sin of omission*** should remove all doubt. Most news sources are ultimately owned by major corporations.

5 Most folks know that the media is liberal controlled, but to my knowledge, even Fox News did not run the Banister story.

6 Internet news provider *WorldNetDaily* ran the story, but no such mention was made by mainstream news outlets. To them — and for the 7% of the population that relies exclusively upon "conventional news" for their daily information — the Banister verdict did not take place.

7 There can never be any doubt left that the quality of our current conventional media has deteriorated to that of Pravda during the era of the Soviet Union.

8 So here's the pure truth not revealed.

9 ***Joe Banister, Former Criminal Investigator for the IRS, acquitted of all four criminal tax counts***

10 Trial began on Tuesday, June 14, 2005 and at approximately 2 p.m., on June 24, on the 14th floor of the Federal Court Building in Sacramento, California, Joe Banister supporters received word that the judge had just been given a note from the jury, and quickly moved from the hallway into the courtroom, where Judge William Shubb announced that the jury had reached a **unanimous decision**.

11 The verdicts were read by the clerk of the court with Judge Shubb presiding: **"Not guilty"**, **"Not guilty"**, **"Not guilty"**, **"Not guilty"**.

12 What were the charges?

13 1) Conspiracy to Defraud the United States, and

14 2) Aiding and Abetting in the

Preparation of False and Fraudulent Returns.

15 The government alleged that Banister had "impeded and impaired the ascertainment, assessment, and collection of tax" and that he had criminally conspired with Redding, CA businessman, Al Thompson in so doing.

16 These charges were related to Joe's association with Walter "Al" Thompson, where Joe, as a CPA, prepared **amended Form 1040X tax returns** for three tax years.

17 These returns were a **calculated protest**, and every effort was made by Al and Joe to adhere to written and verbal guidance they sought and received from the IRS.

18 Key evidence in the trial were **two video tapes**. The first tape — two hours in length — had been filmed at Al Thompson's business, **Cencal Aviation**, in July of 2000.

19 Mr. Thompson had researched the law and drew the concluded that **he was not an "employer" as defined within Title 26 — the income tax code — nor was he required to withhold money from the paychecks of those people who worked for him.**

20 Thompson called the meeting to tell his 25 employees of this decision to stop withholding from their paychecks, and invited Joe Banister, **former IRS Criminal Investigation Division** (CID) **special agent**, to assist him in communicating his decision to his employees.

21 In viewing the content of the tape that greatly favored Mr. Banister, one would have to question the judgment of the government.

22 The tape covered a lot of ground. In it, Joe Banister explained how he came to be employed by the IRS and what caused him to resign after nearly 6 years. He emphasized that **he was not there to tell people what to think or what to do** but simply **to tell them what he learned and what he was doing about his discovery.**

23 Banister was asking the government to rebut the claims of his analysis which consisted of the 95-page report he submitted to his supervisor, Robert Gorini, with the request that it "**go to the top**" for a response. Their re-

sponse was *administrative leave* and Mr. Banister's inevitable resignation, and that the government **would not address his questions**. This constitutes a **commercial dishonor**.

24 The defense began arguing early Friday morning and played the "**Gorini deposition**" to start.

25 The judge gave a 15 minute recess and upon everyone's return, directed defense attorney Jeffrey Dickstein to proceed. Mr. Dickstein surprised and shocked everyone by quietly announcing, **"Your Honor, the defense rests"**.

26 The judge stared at him for several seconds as if speechless.

27 Finally, he asked Dickstein why — knowing the calendar of events — had he not given the court prior knowledge about this short defense and his premature resting.

28 The judge *just knew in his heart* that the defense was going to present witnesses, and expected Mr. Banister to testify on his own behalf. Now, with the defense suddenly and unexpected complete, there was a hole in the day's schedule.

29 No problem. There were Rule 29 issues to discuss outside the presence of the jury and the all-important need to come to agreement on the subject of jury instructions.

30 The jury had been dismissed until Tuesday morning so as to allow plenty of time to complete business before bringing the jury back into the box.

31 Judge Shubb said many interesting, perhaps curious things during the week. Once, he uttered, "the law is uncertain".

32 Another time he declared that no one reads the Internal Revenue Code from cover to cover, and that anyone who claims to have done so, should be in the "nuthouse".

33 The other tape was a deposition of Banister's former IRS Manager in Washington, D.C., Robert Gorini, who retired from the IRS in early 2000, a few weeks after Mr. Banister resigned from the IRS — taken by Banister's attorney, Jeffrey Dickstein.

34 Mr. Gorini had nothing but good things to say about Joe's character, his work as an IRS criminal investigator and many other areas.

35 The very last question Dickstein asked Gorini, was *"Can you name the law that requires Mr. Banister to file income tax returns and pay income taxes?"* Mr. Gorini replied that he could not.

36 Joseph Banister's efforts to get the government to answer his concerns and questions about the income tax include several trips to the nation's capital, where he has often been accompanied by many others who hold similar views, including former IRS revenue agent Sherry Jackson and former IRS revenue officer John Turner.

37 *"The care of human life and happiness, and not their destruction, is the first and only legitimate object of good government."— Thomas Jefferson.*

38 May the grace of our Lord Jesus Christ be with you all. Amen.

CHAPTER 39

AS an **Educator** I am aware of the definition of **"taxpayer."**

2 A taxpayer is **"any person subject to any internal revenue tax."** — *IRS Code 7701(1)(14).*

3 I am aware of the **Collective Entity Rule** and its application to the definition of the word **person**.

4 The word **person** in the IRS Code means an **"individual, trust, estate, partnership, association, company or corporation."** — *IRS Code 7701(a).*

5 Under the Supreme Court **Collective Entity Rule** those entities defined as **persons** in the definition of persons are required to file and pay the Federal Income Tax and have no constitutionally guaranteed rights.

6 But as a **natural person**, I do have constitutionally guaranteed rights. Therefore I am not the **person** defined as a **taxpayer** in section 7701(a) of the IRS Code.

7 I am aware of **section 7806(b)** of the IRS Code that states that "no descriptive matter relating to the contents of the [IRS Code] be given any legal effect . . . before its enactment into law."

8 I therefore demand that the IRS provide the citation and the date when Title 26 was enacted into law throughout the 50 states, claiming that it was not.

9 Sometime before I reached the legal age wherein I could enter into contracts (18), I applied for and received a **Social Security Number**.

10 I mistakenly checked the box indicating that I was a **U.S. citizen** within the meaning of **26 CFR §1-1.1(c)** — *"Every person born or naturalized in the United States and subject to its jurisdiction is a citizen."*

11 Over the years employers asked me for my **Social Security Number** as part of the paper work to be completed before I was hired — as suggested on the Social Security card which states, "SHOW this to your employer".

12 Before I was hired I was asked to fill out a **W-4** form and list my deductions, which I voluntarily did do.

13 Over the years I voluntarily filed many **1040 Individual Income Tax forms** with the Fed-

eral United States Government. On each I placed my **Social Security Number** to identify myself.

14 Recently I have been studying the voluntary nature of Social Security, the Federal Income Tax, and Internal Revenue Code, and have come to the conclusion that I no longer choose to voluntarily participate in any government programs other than Social Security retirement insurance which I now collect.

15 I have severed all other contractual relationships that have existed between me and the Federal United States and its agencies.

16 The original **Social Security contracts** between me and the Federal Government were entered into before I was of the legal age to enter into contracts (18) therefore the contracts are unenforceable and void.

17 I was born in the United States, in the Maine Republic not within the boundaries of the United States as defined in Article 1, Section 8 of the Constitution of the United States.

18 Those **adhesive contracts** defined me as a **person** within the meaning of the IRS Code — as an "individual, a trust, estate, partnership, association, company or corporation." — *IRS Code 7701(a)*.

19 This definition of me is absurd as it is obvious to all who know me that I am a **natural person**, not a **legal fiction** as defined in the IRS code 7701(a). It is self-evident that I am not a **legal fiction — a strawman —** therefore the contracts are unenforceable and void.

20 All contracts between me and the IRS are based upon me being defined as a **taxpayer** as "any **person** subject to any internal revenue tax." — *IRC 7701(1)(14)*.

21 I am a **natural person** outside of the taxing authority of the United States as defined in the Constitution.

22 To hold otherwise is a direct violation of the Supreme Court's **Collective Entity Rule**. The adhesive contracts between me and the Federal Government are therefore unenforceable and void.

23 The contracts between me and the Federal Government (wherein I agreed to turn over a

portion of my money to the Federal Government) are unenforceable because to force me to turn over any portion of my money to the Federal Government would create a condition of **slavery** and **involuntary servitude** which are unconstitutional according to the 13th Amendment and therefore void.

24 The adhesive contracts between me and the Federal Government are fraudulent because they violate the Supreme Court's **Collective Entity Rule** placing me in the category of a **legal fiction** which I am not.

25 By withholding the definitions of **citizen**, **person**, and **taxpayer** the government harmed me and created a condition of fraud because that information was withheld from me and not fully disclosed.

26 Had I known this withheld information I would not have entered into the adhesive contracts with the government. Therefore the contracts between me and the Federal Government are fraudulent, unenforceable and void.

27 It is obvious to me that the IRS Code, Title 26 is not positive law throughout the 50 united States because that is what the code says in **IRC 7806(b)**. — *See title page, and pages III and VII of Volume Thirteen.*

28 This confirms that there is no law authorizing the government to demand any portion of my earnings from my labor and establishes the fact that participating in the IRS system is voluntary and established and enforced by contract.

29 I am not engaged in nor is any of my income derived from alcohol, tobacco, or firearms.

30 As my **REMEDY** I demand that the IRS change my **Individual Master File** to the non-taxpayer designation **MFR-01, "not required to file"**.

31 May the grace of our Lord Jesus Christ be with you all. Amen.

CHAPTER 40

UNDER the Supreme Court's **"Collective Entity Rule"** first stated in *Hale v. Henkle (1906)*, each **entity** named in IRC 7701(a) is a **"person"** created on paper, a **"strawman,"** a **legal person** that has no constitutional rights, whereas I am a **natural person** instead.

2 The difference between a **"person"** and a **natural person** is stated in *Hale v. Henkle, that*:

3 *"The individual may stand upon his constitutional rights as a citizen. He is entitled to carry on his private business in his own way. His power to contract is unlimited. He owes no duty to the State or to his neighbors to divulge his business, or to open his doors to an investigation, so far as it may tend to incriminate him.* ***He owes no duty to the State, since he receives nothing therefrom, beyond the protection of his life and property.*** *His rights are such as existed by the* ***Law of the Land*** *long antecedent to the organization of the State (natural common Law), and can only be taken from him by* ***due process of law*** *and in accordance with the Constitution."*

4 I willingly admit that it was through my action that I mistakenly changed from being a **natural person** to a **person** when I asked for and received a **Social Security Number** from the Federal United States and used that number over the years in filing **Individual Income Tax Returns** to identify myself.

5 I willingly admit that I erred when I asked for and received a **Social Security Number** and I equally erred when over the years I filed **Individual Income Tax Returns** as an **"IRS Code individual"** which I was not.

6 My defense for my mistaken actions is that I was never provided with **full disclosure** from any agency or representative of the Federal Government on the meaning and affect of my actions. Therefore I acted upon incomplete information to my detriment and was defrauded because I was never given **full disclosure in good faith**.

7 It is a long established principle of law that fraud has no statute of limitations and cancels every contract.

8 The term **natural person** is

used in at least 14 different sections of the IRS Code (42, 72, 141, 163, 264, 489, 954, 1271, 1272, 2613, 5801, 5848, 6049, 6231).

9 Notice the pertinent parts of **IRC 141(b)(6)** - PRIVATE BUSINESS USE DEFINED.

10 *"In general, the term **private business** means a trade or business carried on by any person other than a government unit; such **use** as a member of the general public shall not be taken into account — any activity carried on by a **person** other than a **natural person** shall be treated as a trade or business. When it is intended that the term **natural person** be made a part of the term **person** in the United States Code, the term **natural person** is made a conspicuous part of such definition."*

11 Clearly we have established that there is a distinction between us as a **natural person** and **person** as defined in **IRS Code 7701(a).**

12 It is self-evident that a **natural person** exists and never disappears.

13 I claim as a **natural person,**

by my very existence my guaranteed rights that stem from both State and Federal Constitutions, and the Bill of Rights, to full due process of law in all my actions.

14 **SUMMARY**

15 The United States presumes to occupy the position of a Sovereign over our actions.

16 By definition, a sovereign is "a person, body, or state in which independent and supreme authority is vested." — *Blacks Law Dictionary, abridged, 6th edition.*

17 We are **natural persons** and not fictitious **persons** defined in **IRS Code 7701(a).**

18 If we were such a person, business entity, or paper creation (strawman) we would be a **person** defined in the IRS Code at 7701(a) even if it meant our demise.

19 The Government is always attempting to re-create us as a **person** whereas we are **natural persons** with constitutionally defined rights, among which is the right to act as ourselves; not represent ourselves or any legal term such as **strawman** that would dilute who we are.

20 I am rebutting the assump-

tion that I am a **person** within the definition of the artful (deceitful) words in the IRS Code. That I exist as a **natural person** is self-evident.

21 As a **natural person** I am neither the subject nor the object of the **Internal Revenue Code** for I am external to the jurisdiction of the **district United States**.

22 We must not overlook the words of our Founding Fathers so well stated in the **Declaration of Independence**:

23 *"We hold these truths to be self-evident, that all men are created equal, that they are endowed by their Creator with certain unalienable rights, that among these are life, liberty and the pursuit of happiness. That to secure these rights, governments are instituted among men, deriving their just powers from the consent of the governed."*

24 For any court in these United States to rule that the Government is sovereign would mean that we as **natural persons** would be its possessions, subjects, and slaves.

25 I reject the Government's assumption that it is sovereign, as a contract dispute involving **fraud** in the inducement, **slavery**, and **involuntary servitude** in the application of the Supreme Court's **Collective Entity Rule**.

26 *"Sovereignty itself is, of course, not subject to law, for it is the author and source of law; but in our system, while sovereign powers are delegated to the agencies of government, **sovereignty itself remains with the people, by whom and for whom all government exists and acts.** And the law is the definition and limitation of power. It is, indeed, quite true that there must always be lodged somewhere, and in some person or body, the authority of final decision; and in many cases of mere administration, the responsibility is purely political, no appeal lying except to the ultimate tribunal or the public judgment, exercised either in the pressure of opinion, or by means of the suffrage."* — *Yick Wo v. Hopkins, 118 US 356 (1886).*

27 I refuse to accept the government's presumption that I am a **person (strawman)** defined in **IRS Code 7701(a).**

28 If I were a **person** within the meaning of the **IRS Code 7701(a)** I would be a creation of the Federal Government and therefore could not bring an action in my own name under my

own authority which I am now doing, because **persons** cannot represent themselves and must be represented by a **representative** called an attorney.

29 IRC 7806(b) of Title 26 clearly states that Title 26 is not "positive law" throughout the **50 united States** and therefore is applicable only in the **Federal Zone** called the United States.

30 By not acknowledging what the Code itself says (that it is not positive law) we are being defrauded and subjected to **slavery** and **involuntary servitude**.

31 The Federal United States Government can't make any laws that apply to anything within any State.

32 The boundaries between the Federal Government and the States are as defined in the Constitution at Article 1, Section 8.

33 I was not born in the constitutionally defined area called the **United States** even though I mistakenly stated that I was.

34 I was born in the continental **United States of the Union**.

35 As a natural person I am not the subject nor the object of any **Internal Revenue Tax law**.

36 May the grace of our Lord Jesus Christ be with you all. Amen.

CHAPTER 41

ON the day you were born your parents gave you a name that is spelled in **upper and lower case letters**.

2 This is your **given name**, the one to which you respond to in all matters concerning you as a **Creature of God** with Rights from God as a **Sovereign Citizen** of the Republic of Maine (etc.), one of the several States of the **Union of States** called the united States of America.

3 Since the **united States of America** was founded on the premise of individual freedom espoused by the Declaration of Independence, the Constitution, and the Bill of Rights, it is up to you to remind yourself of **who you are**, and what your responsibilities to yourself are.

4 Only you can declare your **God-given Rights**.

5 Since only **entities** that the government creates can be **directly taxed**, the state and federal government created a strawman — **an artificial corporate you** — in their databases under the Uniform Commercial Code.

6 This is significant and has been used to trick, mislead, and confuse you into doing things you **as a strawman** would not have done had you **as a sovereign Citizen** known these differences.

7 And, this has been going on now for more than seventy years since Roosevelt and his "New Deal" in 1933, before we were born.

8 The government created a **fictitious "person"** having the same name as yours which it can directly tax.

9 The Secretary of State in each state maintains a listing of business names (*business corporations*) and individual names (*individual corporations*) upon which commercial liens can be registered under the Uniform Commercial Code.

10 The state is referring to the **"individual you"** — your fictitious strawman — the corporate **"fictitious you"** under commercial law — rather than the **"natural you"** under the laws of nature and nature's God.

11 There are rules of precedence under the UCC whereby the first **"natural person"** or first **"corporate person"** to register a claim against your fictitious

corporate name in the UCC database will be **reimbursed first**.

12 Some people have registered a lien against their own **corporate fictitious name** claiming full rights to all the property and assets their corporate fictitious name owns so that if a third party attempts to use the state's UCC system and the courts to put a lien against them, the third party can't collect in the courts because **the natural man** who owns no property in the public domain will have a **superceding lien** against his strawman's **otherwise taxable property**.

13 This is called **"UCC Redemption"** — or "Commercial Redemption" for short.

14 Take a close look at any paper money you might have.

15 Notice at the very top it reads **"Federal Reserve Note"**.

16 What is a note? A note is a **promise to pay**.

17 A note is not **currency** with intrinsic value that can be traded for silver or gold — which is the only **currency (money)** the government is constitutionally authorized to issue.

18 A note is a **debt instrument**, a debit against the United States held by the ultimate owner of the **debt** the note represents — those who own the **private non-federal** Federal Reserve Bank — not even the Federal Government much less you and me.

19 This artificial **corporate "person"** is your **shadow strawman**. It follows you wherever you go. A revealing song of that era was *"Me and My Shadow"*.

20 Every thing you do is to **accommodate** your shadow strawman, not you.

21 Yet you respond to those things as though they were intended for you and not for your strawman, and in doing so you neglect to reserve your Rights as a sovereign **Citizen of the "united States"** having God given rights.

22 There is a simple way to **"reserve your rights"** and avoid further misunderstandings in the future.

23 Article 1, Section 10 of the U.S. Constitution says, *"No State shall . . . pass any . . . Law impairing the Obligation of Contracts . . ."*

24 This clause establishes the foundation of how to **protect**

your assets from taxes and government seizure using trusts.

25 The Uniform Commercial Code (UCC) prevents us from being **commercially coerced** into signing a contract that we would not sign if we had **true free agency.** If we are forced to sign an **adhesion contract** out of necessity under protest or with prejudice, then we can **preserve our rights** under the U.S. Constitution.

26 UCC 1-207 (PERFORMANCE OR ACCEPTANCE UNDER RESERVATION OF RIGHTS) states:

27 *A party who with explicit **reservation of rights** performs or promises performance or assents to performance in a manner demanded or offered by the other party does not thereby prejudice the rights reserved. Such words as "without prejudice," "under protest" or the like are sufficient.*

28 If it becomes necessary to assert your rights in court when the point is raised, here is an informed way you can explain what you mean when you claimed *"without prejudice" or "under protest".*

29 "I am exercising the **remedy** provided for me in the Uniform Commercial Code which says that I cannot be compelled to perform under any contract that I have not **knowingly, voluntarily** and **intentionally** entered with **full disclosure.**

30 "This **remedy** notifies all administrative agencies of government that I do not accept the liability associated with the compelled benefits of any unrevealed commercial agreement contract."

31 The Uniform Commercial Code is **Admiralty Law** that has come ashore. The **"without prejudice"** clause is the **window** that enables you to assert your 7th Amendment guarantee of access to the **Common Law.**

32 According to *Anderson's UCC annotated*, you can only reserve the rights you have so it's a good idea to be **explicit** about your **"domicile Citizenship"** and deny any **presumption of "14th Amendment citizenship".**

33 **NO NATURAL PERSON DIRECT TAX**

32 The IRS Tax Guide asks, *"who is required to file a 1040 form?"* The IRS Tax Guide an-

swers, *"all citizens of the United States no matter where they are located."*

33 Here then is how the IRS defines *the United States* in Title 26, Subtitle F, Chapter 79, Section 7001, DEFINITIONS . . .

34 *The term "United States" when used in a geographical sense includes only the* **States** *and the* **District of Columbia.** — 7701(a)(9).

35 *The term "State" shall be construed to include the* **District of Columbia,** *where such construction is necessary to carry out the provisions of this title [meaning title 26].* — 7701(a)(10).

36 Substituting the definition for the term *'State'* into the definition for *'United States'* we arrive at this . . .

37 *The term "United States" when used in a geographical sense includes only (the* **District of Columbia)** *and the* **District of Columbia.** *(curious, but true).*

38 If you weren't born in the **District of Columbia** then you are **not** a **"citizen of the United States"** required to file a 1040 Tax Return. You are a **Citizen of the united States of America.**

39 If you have ever *declared* yourself to be a **"citizen of the United States"** (*a 14th Amendment "person" = a federal corporation that can be directly taxed*) then you must *rescind this declaration by affidavit* — or remain a **taxpayer** to the IRS, instead.

40 An informed way to register your **affirmed Declaration of Independence** in the **public record** is to file your declaration as a **UCC-1 Statement** with the **Secretary of State** of your State.

41 May the grace of our Lord Jesus Christ be with you all. Amen.

Above All

Above all powers,
    Above all kings.
Above all nature,
    And all created things.
Above all wisdom,
    And all the ways of man;

  You were here before the world began.

Above all kingdoms,
    Above all thrones.
Above all wonders,
    The world has ever known.
Above all wealth,
    And treasures of the earth;

  There's no way to measure what You're worth.

Crucified,
    Laid behind a stone.
You lived to die,
    Rejected and alone.
Like a rose,
    Trampled on the ground;

  You took the fall,
    And thought of me;

    Above all.

EPISTLE TO THE AMERICANS I
What you don't know about the Income Tax

EPISTLE TO THE AMERICANS II
What you don't know about American History

EPISTLE TO THE AMERICANS III
What you don't know about Money

Made in the USA
Monee, IL
10 March 2022